# FROM REFRESHING TO REVIVAL

# from
# *Refreshing*

# to
# REVIVAL

## Terry Virgo
### David Holden
### John Hosier

**KINGSWAY PUBLICATIONS**
EASTBOURNE

ISBN 0 85476 594 8

Design and layout by Pinnacle Creative Ltd for
KINGSWAY PUBLICATIONS LTD
Lottbridge Drove, Eastbourne, E Sussex, BN23 6NT.
Printed in Great Britain,
by arrangement with Bookprint Creative Services.

# Contents

# Introction

**A**round the world in this last two years christian magazines and even secular newspapers have been reporting a remarkable new demonstration of the Holy Spirit's activity in local churches.

Many have called it a 'season of refreshing', others 'a time of renewal'. Some have even called it 'revival'. Is it revival? Surely we must reply that so far it lacks a number of the features usually associated with full revival. Nevertheless, there is a new intensity of the Holy Spirit's presence in many churches and individual christian lives. Literally hundreds of thousands have now travelled across the world to such places as Airport Vineyard, Toronto, and other similar centres where God is meeting with His people in remarkable ways.

Where do we go from here? Though we are reluctant to call this current move of the Holy Spirit 'revival' we are still eager to press on to the full flood. These chapters are offered as an encouragement to help us firstly to recognise what is taking place amongst us. Secondly, we want to encourage wise stewardship and administration of the Holy Spirit's activity in the churches. Thirdly, we hope to point the way forward to the full-scale revival for which we all long. The inroads of secularism are now so great in modern society that the culture is profoundly ungodly. Only a sweeping revival can arrest the downward drift and bring the changes so desperately needed. May this book inspire you to continue drinking of the water of life and seeing the longed-for revival that must come for the glory of Christ.

My personal thanks and appreciation go to the sterling work done by Mary Austin as she has reshaped material, most of which came first in the form of preaching. It is because of her endeavours that this book is now in your hands.

Terry Virgo

Restore us again, O God our Saviour,
and put away your displeasure towards us.
Will you be angry with us for ever?
Will you prolong your anger through all generations?
Will you not revive us again,
that your people may rejoice in you?
Show us your unfailing love, O Lord,
and grant us your salvation.

Ps. 85:4–7

# A fresh outpouring

TERRY VIRGO

The account of Peter and Cornelius in Acts 10 marks the turning point in the history of the early church. It helped the christians understand who they were, what their calling was and where the frontiers of that calling were. It also has a lot to say to us now that we're experiencing this fresh outpouring of the Holy Spirit.

## The fresh initiative was from God

The breakthrough into Cornelius' household didn't come out of a strategy meeting of the apostles. They didn't think, 'Now we'll go to the Gentiles'. Peter was unwilling to associate with anything 'unclean' and when the apostles heard that he'd been into a Gentile home, they were very uneasy. The initiative was from God, not men. He was saying, 'It's time for another breakthrough of the Spirit'. And they were taken completely by surprise.

Church history can only truly be understood in the context of revivals. There has never been steady development — any more than there was in the Old Testament. You can't project a graph into the future and say, 'This is where we are now, so ultimately we'll be over there'. Certainly, we can have our short and long term goals, but church history is wrapped up in the sovereignty of God and in Christ who governs His church. Jesus sits as King and declares, 'Now I'll do a new thing.'

Great Britain was in a terrible state before the great Weşleyian revival. You couldn't have projected what would happen because God suddenly intervened. Then in another period of spiritual bankruptcy, God moved in through William Booth and the Salvation Army. They began churches around the world because God blew on them.

Church history has always had these flood times. The Puritans didn't believe in the natural progression of the Kingdom of God. They said that it would spread and triumph through powerful operations of the Holy Spirit. Suddenly God would surge in, revival would break out and Jesus would be revealed as Lord. Here, in Acts 10, we see such an occasion. The church was making excellent progress in spite of persecution, and suddenly God said, 'It's time for the next phase. You're going to the Gentiles.'

Following his visit to Cornelius' house, Peter returned to Jerusalem and was met by opposition. 'The circumcised believers criticised him and said, "You went into the house of uncircumcised men and ate with them"' (Acts 11:2,3). Peter had obeyed the Holy Spirit, but the brothers whom he loved and respected had not received this fresh revelation from God.

Peter knew that as an apostle of God he was called to honour the leaders of the church and keep it united. It wasn't his desire to run off and start some new thing, yet God was clearly doing a new thing and he couldn't abandon it.

Human response is crucial when God moves in a fresh way. We're responsible to stay flexible and catch the wind of the Spirit. Church history tells us that people often failed to allow God to breathe new life into the church, which meant that men like Wesley and Booth were forced to move outside the mainstream church. This is tragic. If we can be flexible when God breathes again, we won't see another splintering. Rather, we'll hold together and enjoy the fresh touch of God.

Every revival has its roots in the authentic. John the Baptist brought a threatening new word for his generation, yet this new word went right back into orthodox Judaism. So God doesn't look down on the sad condition of the church in our nation and think, 'Forget the church. I'll go outside it. Perhaps I'll take on the New Age movement. They're more open'. He's committed to His church, to those He's called and loves.

It's amazing what people experience in just this one chapter of Acts. There's prayer, a trance, a vision, an audible voice, the Spirit's leading, an angel and the Spirit falling on people. This is church life just like we know it! People don't often go into trances. If you get one of those, you'd better see the elders quick! What about visions? Peter didn't experience a vague dreamy kind of thing. Heaven came down and requirements were made of him. Then there's the audible voice. I wonder if it was familiar to Peter, the same one that he'd heard over the previous three years.

Next the Spirit spoke to him and made it clear that he should go. We need to rediscover the Spirit's ability to speak to us direct. Jeremiah had known God for years, then one day God told him, 'Write in a book all the words I have spoken to you' (Jer. 30:2). It would never have occurred to Jeremiah to do this, but he had a relationship with the Spirit and followed the Spirit's leading.

Christians need to study the Scriptures and read books, but christianity was never meant to be a 'booky' religion. God has chosen the poor, the weak, the foolish and the things that are not — many of whom live in poor countries and simply haven't had the chance to be 'booky'. But even those of us who do have access to books must learn that God doesn't want us to rely on our study, but to listen so that we can know Him more intimately. Since I've been touched by this present outpouring of the Spirit, I've found that I've become more keen to read theology than ever before.

Then there was an angel — Cornelius saw that. Certainly, we mustn't cultivate an appetite for the weird, but we must acknowledge the reality of angels. Finally, the Spirit fell while Peter was speaking to Cornelius' household. Recalling the event, Peter said, 'As I began to speak' (Acts 11:15). From his 'preacher's perspective' he'd hardly got started when the Spirit came. And that visitation, like the experience at Pentecost was beyond his control.

It's important to note that the angel told Cornelius to, 'Send to Joppa for Simon who is called Peter. He will bring you a message through which you and all your household will be saved' (Acts 11:13,14). We're not entering a phase in which everything is so supernatural that we don't need words any more. Cornelius and his family needed to hear the gospel. Peter may have thought that he'd explained very little about Jesus. But he'd obviously given enough content to lock his hearers into the truth before the Spirit overwhelmed them (Acts 10:37–43).

Peter's explanation of what happened in Joppa was full of references to the supernatural. The early church embraced what the unbeliever would find almost impossible to understand. We mustn't reduce the church to a system of theology and mental activity. It's a supernatural creation. Christians are born from above; they're new creations in Christ. We were dead and have come alive. A supernatural people should be at home in a supernatural dimension.

## It could be rationally explained

We read, 'Peter began and explained everything to them precisely as it had happened' (Acts 11:4). It's important to note: you can be involved with strange supernatural phenomena and yet still be able to explain what's happening. If you love other christians, you won't just tell them, 'You want to experience this, then you'll know how good it is' or 'I can't really communicate what happened, but it was wonderful'. That's not very helpful. Even though Peter's story was full of supernatural things, he still explained what happened in an orderly way. With certain limitations, we must do the same.

In his gospel Luke says, 'Since I myself have carefully investigated everything from the beginning, it seemed good also to me to write an orderly account' (Luke 1:3). Luke had listened to other servants of the Word. He'd checked the facts and now he wanted to set them out in order. Having said this, he starts talking about an old man who saw an angel and was struck dumb; an old woman who became pregnant; a virgin who conceived and angels in the sky. This is other worldly, but Luke can still investigate it and tell us in sequence exactly what happened.

We mustn't get the idea that once we get into the supernatural we kiss our brains goodbye. What goes on may be outside our normal realm of understanding, but we can say, 'This happened, then that did'. We can tell people why we believe and what Jesus has done for us.

Although our modern world lusts after occult phenomena, it has great difficulty with anything supernatural. Perhaps the sadder thing is that many christians struggle over the supernatural and fail to see it as part of the church's inheritance. We must try hard to bring them into revelation of these things.

When I was at Bible College in the 1960s I arranged for Arthur Wallis to come and speak to the students about revival. It was a marvellous evening. He illustrated his talk by referring to the revival that was then taking place in Indonesia and recounted stories of breathtaking miracles. The following day there were problems because some of the students didn't want to think that supernatural things took place. They didn't want to hear about that kind of thing. I was grieved.

That evening I happened to be at Westminster Chapel where Dr. Martyn Lloyd-Jones was preaching. He was talking about

Philip in Samaria — the gospel, the power and the signs. I was drinking it in, thinking how similar some of the content of his message was to what I'd heard the previous night.

I was so stirred that after the meeting I decided to talk to him. I told him what had happened after Arthur Wallis had spoken and he found that interesting. Then he asked me, 'How many points did I say that I had this evening?' I said, 'Three'. He continued, 'And how many points did I preach?' I replied, 'You only preached on one point'. 'That's right' he said. Then he laughed, looked at a little pile of papers on his table and said, 'Those notes will do for next week. God came on me while I was preaching'.

I explained my dilemma to him. 'I want to be orthodox and respect truth,' I said. 'But when we start looking for more, we're told, "You mustn't search after these things". But you were preaching what I believe in — signs, wonders, miracles — although we're not seeing many of them. I just believe that they're part of what God has for us.' He replied, 'The greatest sin in the evangelical church is this: we want to put God in a little box and tell Him what He is and isn't permitted to do. Remember the present continuous — ask, and go on asking; seek and go on seeking; knock and go on knocking. Keep seeking after God, because He'll display His power if you ask Him.' He was so encouraging.

We must remain open to God and resist the temptation to tell Him what He can and can't do. It's His church and we mustn't shut Him into our own limited previous experience. Sometimes we may find it hard to describe what's happened to us, but we must try to explain it as far as we can.

On the day of Pentecost 'Peter stood up with the Eleven' to preach (Acts 2:14). I'd always imagined a group of men all standing together with Peter slightly in front. Now I wonder if he was the only one standing when he said, 'These men are not drunk, as you suppose' (Acts 2:15)! But in the midst of what was happening there was a word of explanation, 'This is what was spoken by the prophet Joel' (Acts 2:16). We experience the Spirit and try to explain what's going on.

## It was confronted with prejudice

The news about Peter's visit reached Jerusalem before Peter did. There's a problem when that happens. 'The apostles and the brothers throughout Judea heard ...' (Acts 11:1). They were probably saying, 'Do you know what Peter's up to now? We thought he was a good brother. But he's been eating with Gentiles and even baptising them.'

Preconceived judgements are often rooted in a genuine fear of God and we mustn't always despise them. When the sheet came down from heaven and Peter was invited to kill and eat from it, he couldn't respond positively. That's because he couldn't identify with the new phase that God was bringing in. He feared God and wanted to continue obeying Him. His motives weren't wrong, they were pure.

We may hear people say, 'I don't think I like this,' but we mustn't jump to the conclusion that they're opposed to it. They may want to look at it more closely and we must love them enough to give them space to do this. Peter had difficulties because he loved God. He'd let Jesus down before and wanted to be faithful now.

If the sheet contained all sorts of animals, we could ask, 'Why didn't Peter simply leave the unclean animals and take the clean ones?' Maybe the association of the two kinds together made it hard for him to take any of them. Down through the ages this has been a problem with the church. We see God do something new, but there are things around it that we don't like and we're tempted to reject it all.

We see a man on the same platform as someone else and think, 'I can't associate with him now that he's aligned himself with that crowd'. Happily, this kind of attitude seems to be fading away, but we do need to be able to weigh what's going on because that's helpful. I've felt really blessed at many meetings where the Spirit has been moving in power. Yet in some of those meetings people have said and done things that I haven't gone along with. On those occasions I mentally set aside what I don't like and praise God for what I do.

It's incredible what He's doing. I left secular work in 1963 and since then I've never seen anything like this move of the Spirit. It's running round the world and God is blessing people in the most wonderful ways. Some of the christians in India wrote down their testimonies. See what you think of them:

'I didn't want to come to the meetings, but once I was down I started to sing. God showed me areas of sin, selfishness and grumbling in me and as I began to ask for forgiveness I felt His arms around me. I didn't want to go back home. I began to enjoy His presence and I wanted Him alone.'

'The Holy Spirit has made me sensitive to sin. He corrects me quickly of wrong thoughts and selfish speech. As I was talking to a friend trying rather forcefully to make my point, the Holy Spirit showed me my arrogance. I quickly apologised.'

'I thought God is not going to work in my life the way He is doing in others. But God did otherwise. He spoke to me about living by the Spirit so powerfully that it has transformed my life and broken all my set patterns of praying, speaking, thinking and even meeting people. Now I realise how little I was living by the Spirit and how much I was living on my own understanding.'

'I came to God feeling defeated and miserable. In all the anxieties of life, God showed me how foolish I had been wasting my time worrying about little needs when my big God was in total charge of my life. I began to laugh when I began to see how secure I was in God.'

At a prayer meeting in the USA an elder's wife suddenly started prancing around and singing, 'I'm a marionette'. The elders stood round looking embarrassed, but afterwards she told us what was happening. Apparently God was saying, 'You don't have to carry those burdens. You're like a puppet. Leave the burdens. I'll carry you and give you life.' All we could see was what was happening on the outside, but God was speaking wonderful truths into her heart.

This happens so often now. You see things going on outwardly and wonder, 'What on earth is all that about?' I've never seen so many strange things in all my life. During two days of prayer and fasting there were drunken men all over the floor, grabbing one another, laughing and having odd pictures. One guy in a meeting in a church in India actually took a jug of cold water and poured it over his head! He still doesn't know why he did it. His wife had to be carried home because she was incapable of walking.

Just before Stoneleigh Bible Week 1994 one of the elders at Church of Christ the King in Brighton preached on the grace of God. At the end of his message he invited those who were going to be working at Stoneleigh to stand. I stood and the elder said to us, 'God bless you'. Everyone sat down and I slumped into my chair and stayed there for the next hour. I could hear people talking and walking around, but I could also hear God. As the building emptied, everything got quieter and quieter and I just sat there, unable to move, with God speaking wonderful things into my heart. My son, Joel sat down next to me and said, 'Are you ready to go home, Dad?' Someone else came along with a bunch of keys wanting to lock up. My wife, Wendy, poked me and said, 'He's dead to the world'. But I wasn't. I was aware of everything that was going on but I just wanted to linger in the presence and love of God. I may not be able to understand it all, but I can explain what I do understand.

I'm so glad that there are positive results from this move of the Spirit. One of the first testimonies I ever heard was, 'Our marriage is better than it ever has been'. A man who was going to leave the church went round apologising to every elder for the pain that he'd caused. He's at the prayer meetings and his life has been transformed. A middle-aged woman who teaches Latin in a school was lying on the floor laughing, shaking and wondering what her pupils would say if they could see her. As she lay there, God asked her, 'What do you want?' She replied, 'I want this school for you.' He said, 'Ask Me for it.' You see, it isn't just laughing and shaking and bodies on floors, it's people hearing things inside: 'I'm freeing you. You don't have to carry that burden any more. I'll carry you.'

Yes, there are some mixtures here and there. I've heard things said in public meetings that I don't agree with. But in the mercy of God I saw so many good things early on that they saved me from distancing myself from what was happening. We can be shocked sometimes: 'What's that doctrine? What's that statement? What's that practice?' Let me encourage you to respect those whom God is powerfully using, to keep listening to biblical truth and to open yourself to this fresh move of the Spirit. Seek truth and Spirit together.

When Peter was invited to kill and eat the animals in the sheet, he replied, 'Surely not, Lord!' (Acts 10:14). He said similar words to Jesus when he tried to rebuke Him for predicting His death (Matt. 16:22). We can't say, 'No' to God. What He calls clean, we must beware of judging and calling unclean.

### It was victorious over prejudice
God was kind to Peter. He was wondering about the meaning of the vision and 'Right then three men ... stopped at the house' (Acts 11:11). That's the providential outworking of God. We don't only arrive at conclusions through our research, but also through the awareness that God orders our steps.

In February 1993 we had a prophetic word at the church in Brighton. God said, 'Prepare yourselves for disruption'. We didn't know what it was all about, but we recognised its authority and took it seriously. God was giving us providential preparation. We've got to take note of these sorts of things. God whispers to us and prepares us — as He did with Peter. All Peter needed to know was, 'Is this You, Lord?' And if we love Jesus, that's all we need to know. We may think, 'This is a bit embarrassing', but if it's really God, who cares?

I was praying for people in one meeting and noticed that a number of elderly folk were coming forward. It really moved me to see them falling into the arms of those behind them. It would have been so easy for them to have thought, 'This move of the Spirit is for the young ones, it's not for me'. But they were there at the front saying, 'Please pray for me'. All they needed to know was, 'Is this You, Lord?' Once they knew it was, they'd go with it.

Peter had been trained for three years to understand when Jesus was present in a situation. Once Jesus told Peter to 'let down the nets for a catch' (Luke 5:4). Now Peter and his fishermen friends had worked hard all night and had caught nothing. But they had to learn that their previous knowledge of fishing wasn't the greatest authority. So Peter said to Jesus, 'Because you say so, I will let down the nets' (Luke 5:5).

On another occasion the disciples were in a boat in a storm and Jesus went out to them on the water. The disciples were terrified. Then Jesus said to them, 'Take courage! It is I. Don't be afraid' (Matt. 14:27). To this, Peter replied, 'Lord, if it's you ... tell me to come to you on the water' (Matt. 14:28).

When the Pharisees confronted the apostles for preaching in the name of Jesus, a man called Gamaliel advised the Pharisees, 'Leave these men alone! Let them go! For if their purpose or activity is of human origin, it will fail. But if it is from God, you will not be able to stop these men; you will only find yourselves fighting against God' (Acts 5:38,39). This may have sounded like wise counsel, but he shouldn't have said, 'Leave well alone' but, 'Research it. Find out what's going on'.

God is moving by His Spirit. We mustn't say, 'Well, it's better than what we were getting before, but let's be wise about it. We'll watch from a distance and see what happens.' If Gamaliel had said, 'Look into this,' the people would have found Jesus. Our nation desperately needs a revelation of God, an outpouring of the Holy Spirit's joy and power. If it's the Lord, let's not pussyfoot around. Let's go!

# Anointing with power

**DAVID HOLDEN**

We've been enjoying wonderful times of refreshing. People have been feeling God's presence, and His power has been moving on their lives. I love being refreshed by God. For me, each meeting is another opportunity to receive a new touch from Him. Of course, I can receive from Him whether I'm in a meeting or not. But I simply want as much refreshing as I can possibly get.

While this is a time of refreshing, it's also a time of empowering. People are testifying, 'As people keep ministering to me, I'm gradually becoming aware of a new power in my life. God is really strengthening and helping me.' If we're going to change the world, we desperately need God's power. We need it to fulfil our calling, to overcome problems, to be effective parents, to be witnesses and to move in signs and wonders. I can't live my life without God's power working within me, but if there's one thing I often feel I lack, it's power.

Behind the shaking, laughing, falling over and the awesome presence of God there should be a power encounter. Paul was weakened by a 'thorn in the flesh', but Jesus refused to remove it. Instead He said, 'My grace is sufficient for you, for my power is made perfect in weakness'. Paul told the Corinthians, 'Therefore I will boast all the more gladly about my weaknesses, so that Christ's power may rest on me. That is why, for Christ's sake, I delight in weaknesses, in insults, in hardships, in persecutions, in difficulties. For when I am weak, then I am strong.' (2 Cor. 12:9,10). Paul didn't want people to think, 'There's the great apostle Paul' but, 'There's the power of Christ resting on a weak man'. He rejoiced in his weaknesses so that people would give the glory to God.

The world presents power as something macho. But power is a Person — the Holy Spirit. In the New Testament, Spirit and power are really one and the same. Before Pentecost the early church had no strength, then the Spirit came and so did the power. God hasn't called you to win through in your own strength, but to live with a Person — the Holy Spirit. It isn't, 'I was baptised in the Spirit ten years ago and that's all I need'. Nor is it, 'Someone prayed for me in a meeting six months ago and I fell over'. They may have been power encounters, but they won't see you through. You get power by living with a Person, yielding to Him, walking by Him, relying on Him every moment of every day. So keep asking others to pray for you, because the more they do that, the more you'll be filled with the Spirit and the more you'll be filled with power.

If you ask me, 'What's happening in this move of the Spirit?' I'd reply, 'I'm observing that more and more people are being empowered by the Holy Spirit and moving in the power of God'. The Lord wants us to be His witnesses and to perform signs and wonders out there in the world. However, we're not going to be able to demonstrate power without if it isn't operating in our lives within. We need to be refreshed, but we also need to be empowered.

Power is often associated with something that's visible. How do you know that Jesus was a man of power? You see Him healing the sick, casting out demons, raising the dead, turning water into wine and stilling the storm. The early church was filled with power. When christians were baptised in the Spirit, Simon the Sorcerer saw something happening and offered the apostles money so that he could move in power as well (Acts 8:18,19). Paul said, 'My message and my preaching were not with wise and persuasive words, but with a demonstration of the Spirit's power' (1 Cor. 2:4). His gospel wasn't just talk, it was power — and the Corinthians saw it. The power was outwardly manifested, but it came from within.

Jesus walked in the Spirit. On one occasion a woman touched the hem of His garment and He was immediately aware that 'power had gone out from him' (Mark 5:30). He wasn't just moving in outward signs and wonders. He was operating from a resource of power that was within. It's dangerous when christians move in power in the public setting, but fail to receive power in their private encounters with God. We all know of people who minister with amazing power to thousands, but whose private lives severely lack integrity. We desperately need the power of God in both our lives and ministries.

## The power within

I think that we need to see the empowering within before we see the empowering without and I'm thrilled at the inner work that God is doing in people's lives. They're learning to respond to the Spirit and drink — something which they didn't do before. In the early days of this time of refreshing, people used to come forward for prayer and speak fervently in tongues while you prayed for them. They'd spend too much time talking and too little receiving. If I came up to you with a glass of water and said, 'I'd like to pour this water into your mouth' you'd have a hard time drinking it if you tried to speak at the same time. But if you opened your mouth and swallowed you'd get the benefit of the water. In the past, we've done lots of talking and discussing, but not much receiving. Now, we're learning how to receive — not with our minds, but in our hearts, and it's strengthening us from within.

This move of the Spirit appears to be outward. We see people falling over, shaking and laughing. But these outward signs are really emerging from what's going on within — the power is so great that either we can't stand, or we can't keep still. The people from the media pick up on the visible manifestations because they're dramatic, but they can't see what's going on inside. That's why we ask people to give testimonies. We're not so much interested in what's going on outwardly, but in what God is doing within.

Every time I do something strange outwardly, it's a result of something that's happening within. The trouble is that you can't see that — which is why it looks so odd. You'll stare at me and think, 'What on earth is he doing that for?' But if you come over and ask me about it afterwards, I can explain it. Sometimes I ask others why they were doing peculiar things in a meeting. When they tell me, I'm always satisfied with the answer because I recognise that the Holy Spirit was at work in them. Jesus said, 'Whoever believes in me ... streams of living water will flow from within him' (John 7:38). What's going on inside must have an outward expression.

In Ephesians 3:16–21, Paul mentions the word 'power' three times in the context of something that's within. Let's look at these three occasions.

### Power in your inner being

First, Paul says, 'I pray that out of his glorious riches, he may strengthen you with power through his Spirit in your inner being' (Eph. 3:16). We need to be strengthened with power because we're prone to weakness and despondency. We give into temptation too easily, or we're lazy. The enemy hits us and we just want to give up. Our society operates on the philosophy, 'If you don't like it, don't do it. If things are tough, do something else — take a pill, get some therapy — you'll get through somehow'. The christian life is a battle. We need to be strong but we haven't got the ability. The power comes from the Holy Spirit within.

Paul says, 'The weapons we fight with are not the weapons of the world. On the contrary, they have divine power to demolish strongholds. We demolish arguments and ever pretension that sets itself up against the knowledge of God, and we take captive every thought to make it obedient to Christ' (2 Cor. 10:4). How do we overcome the enemy? Not by human power, but by divine power. This power is within us, as Paul makes abundantly clear, 'We have this treasure in jars of clay to show that this all-surpassing power is from God and not from us' (2 Cor. 4:7). We test the strength of this power when everything on the outside is in turmoil.

Paul went through a desperate time. 'We were under great pressure,' he said, 'far beyond our ability to endure, so that we despaired even of life. Indeed, in our hearts we felt the sentence of death. But this happened that we might not rely on ourselves but on God, who raises the dead' (2 Cor. 1:8,9). When things came against him, he didn't give in because he knew that he had an inner strength to overcome them. 'We are hard pressed on every side, but not crushed; perplexed, but not in despair; persecuted, but not abandoned; struck down, but not destroyed' (2 Cor. 4:8,9).

You need the power of the Spirit as much as Paul did and God wants you to go forward at meetings to be filled again and again. As you do this, you'll discover that His treasure is in you, His earthen vessel, and that people will begin to notice a new power in you. Paul didn't say, 'I can do everything,' but, 'I can do everything through him who gives me strength' (Phil. 4:13). We need to be 'strengthened with power'. So when you're at a meeting, don't go forward for prayer with the idea of falling over. Go to receive power. You may fall over, you may not. That isn't the issue. You need power for the week that lies ahead.

Christians tend to be too soft, apologetic and cautious. We have a sentimental view of Jesus, when He's confident, robust and powerful. He was so strengthened with power that He was able to take on everyone and overcome them all. At one time some Pharisees advised Him to escape because Herod was out to kill Him. Jesus replied to them, 'Go tell that fox, "I will drive out demons and heal people today and tomorrow, and on the third day I will reach my goal"' (Luke 13:32). This so-called sweet, mild, weak Jesus was saying, 'That old fox isn't pulling the shots. You go tell the king what he can do.' That's powerful. Our sentimental Jesus doesn't appear in the Scriptures.

It's the same with the early church. Hollywood often portrays the first century as a lot of sick, weak and pathetic people holding candles and singing *Ave Maria*. But they were powerful. The same robustness that was in Jesus was in them and should be in us too. God wants to conform us to the image of His Son (Rom. 8:29). Jesus wasn't wishy-washy, and we shouldn't be like that either. 'The righteous are as bold as a lion' (Prov. 28:1).

John the Baptist said, '(Jesus) will baptise you with the Holy Spirit and with fire' (Luke 3:16). This move of the Spirit is putting fire into the church. It's strengthening us with power in our inner being, enabling us to believe God for more and to do greater things in His name. God is waking us up to the strength that we have through the Spirit. We will not be ignored in the end. There will be revival. But we can't do everything that God wants us to do without His power within.

Many of us were baptised in the Holy Spirit but have since been asking, 'Where's the power in my life? Do I need a separate anointing?' No. When you received the Spirit you also received the anointing (1 John 2:27). Up to now, I think that we've accepted the baptism in the Spirit and speaking with tongues as the norm. But I believe that what we're experiencing now is what God wanted us to experience when we were filled with the Spirit in the first place.

Some of us are trying to divorce the baptism of the Spirit from this current move of the Spirit. 'I don't think I want to get into all this weird stuff' we think. 'I might do something strange.' The baptism of the Spirit gives us the power to live right, but we mustn't be satisfied with that. There's a coming upon and an empowering within. The same Spirit who anointed us wants to flow in, remove our dryness and refresh others through us.

This move of the Spirit of God isn't for certain people, it's for everybody because everybody needs power within. So if you go to a meeting and someone says, 'Who wants a fresh touch of the Spirit?' don't think, 'Should I go forward today? Maybe I should hold back and let others receive.' Stand up and get prayed for!

### Power for revelation

Just as we need power to be strengthened in our inner being, so we need power to receive revelation of God's love. Paul says, 'And I pray that you, being rooted and established in love, may have power, together with all the saints, to grasp how wide and long and high and deep is the love of Christ' (Eph. 3:17,18). The modern western mind thinks that it can grasp God's love through intellect. But that's not possible because it's 'love that surpasses knowledge'. To know God's love, we need power from the Holy Spirit.

Some christians find that their love for God grows cold as the years go by. They hear teaching about the cross but it doesn't move them any more. They need a restoration of love for God, and it doesn't come from analysis, sentiment, or even repentance. It comes through the Spirit. They need to ask Him to reveal the love of God to them again. Paul said, 'I pray that you may have power'. Maybe we should do just that — pray for one another that we might have power to grasp the greatness of God's love.

Of course, we don't leave our brains at home when we come into meetings where God is moving. We need to understand God's love with our minds, but we also need to receive it in our hearts. Many people question, 'How can I do that?' At the beginning of this move of the Spirit I found it difficult to receive simply because I was attempting to understand what was going on through my intellect. I was trying to analyse everything and it was hopeless. I came in late to one Sunday meeting and couldn't get into what was happening because I wasn't letting the Spirit touch my heart. I was just watching some of the congregation do strange things. Then I began to learn how to drink and to allow the Spirit to give me revelation.

Paul says, 'The Spirit searches all things, even the deep things of God. For who among men knows the thoughts of a man except the man's spirit within him? In the same way no-one knows the thoughts of God except the Spirit of God. We have not received the spirit of the world but the Spirit who is from God, that we may understand what God has freely given us' (1 Cor. 2:10–12). None of us will ever understand this move of the Spirit through our own faculties — our intellect or observation. We'll understand it only through the Spirit's revelation.

We can't receive this fresh anointing through our intellect and no one else can give it to us. We receive through our hearts. How do we do that? We pray that the Spirit within us will help us. For the first time in my life I've begun to learn about receiving with my heart. That's come through the work of the Holy Spirit.

## Power for faith

Paul continues, '(He) is able to do immeasurably more than all we ask or imagine, according to his power that is at work within us' (Eph. 3:20). The Holy Spirit within us causes us to believe God for great things. According to this verse, faith is linked with the power that's at work within us. The more we're filled with the Spirit, the more power we will have, the greater our faith will be and the more things will happen. We need to be filled with the Spirit who is the source of power and faith.

I'm a very cautious person, but I know that if I'm going to reach out in signs and wonders, I'll have to take risks. I need the Spirit to give me faith to do this. When people came to Jesus for healing, He could often see into their hearts and recognise the presence or absence of faith. Sometimes He told people, 'Your faith has made you well' and He was often disappointed at the lack of His disciples' faith. God wants us to exercise more faith. It doesn't come through some mystical experience, but through the Word (Rom. 10:17) and the power of the Spirit within us.

If we have the power of God within us, we can do things that we can't do in our own strength. Maybe you're in the grip of pornography, smoking, alcohol or some other habit. 'I love Jesus' you say. 'I don't want to be doing this, but I just can't help myself.' Well if you're a christian you can because God gives you the power to stop it. You 'can to everything through him who gives (you) strength' (Phil. 4:13).

Paul tells us that, 'We died to sin' and that 'anyone who has died has been freed from sin' (Rom. 6:2,7). We may think, 'I'm not free from sin' but we are. God has given us the power within to overcome it. The trouble is that we so often choose not to exercise that power. God knows that if we live from the Spirit within, we can stop sinning. It may be a struggle, but He's given us the power to resist all temptation. So if you're battling with sin, ask God to do immeasurably more than all you ask or imagine and draw on the power that's at work in you.

As this move of the Spirit has continued I've found that I've been believing God for greater and greater things. His power is coming upon me and the dreams that I've had for my local church are increasing. God wants to do for us, 'More than we'd ask or imagine, far beyond our wildest dreams'. He wants to fill us with His Spirit and give us faith that He's going to do something remarkable in the UK. Let's receive more of His power and believe Him for huge breakthrough.

### The power without
The power to witness
In view of what's currently going on in our meetings, many of us are wondering whether we should be inviting non-

christians to them. I was praying about this one day. 'Lord,' I said, 'I can't imagine my neighbours ever coming into these meetings.' He replied, 'Well they're not coming to them anyway!' I eventually decided, 'What have I got to lose by asking them along?'

So let's invite non-christians to our meetings. Some who have come really have encountered God in a remarkable way and we must expect this to happen. What we're experiencing is going to tumble out into society anyway, so we may as well let people get a taste of it by encouraging them to join us now.

The issue isn't, 'Let's get this move of the Spirit over so we can get back to normal evangelism'. God wants every part of church life to be affected by the Spirit's present activity — evangelism included. In 1994 there were probably more evangelistic projects set up than ever before. Certainly, God blessed these projects and we were all involved in them, but by the end of 1994 few people were talking about them. Everyone was talking about what we didn't plan — this new move of the Spirit.

At the end of the day, what's going to get the job done isn't just new training, more projects, new methods, or more endeavour — essential though these things may be. We've got to wake up and say, 'Isn't God trying to say something to us? Maybe that project wasn't quite as successful as we made it out to be. It wasn't quite the event of the decade.' This move of the Spirit is bringing a whole new dimension to evangelism and I'm convinced that if we get repeatedly filled with the Spirit we'll become increasingly evangelistic. Didn't

Jesus say, 'You will receive power when the Holy Spirit comes on you; and you will be my witnesses' (Acts 1:8)? We're not in 'receiving mode' with evangelism on one side. We're inviting the Spirit to fill us more and more to be Jesus' witnesses.

Two friends and I were returning home from a powerful ministry trip in Devon. After about two hours' driving we stopped off at a pub. Ray and I went up to the bar to order our drinks while Mike, who was full of the Spirit, walked up to the one customer and said, 'Hi, I'm Mike. What's your name?' 'Sean' he replied. As they talked, Mike discovered that a few months earlier Sean's thirteen year-old son had been killed outside his home, with the result that Sean was really open to the things of God and had even gone along to some christian meetings. After a while, Mike offered to pray for Sean. As he did so, Sean's eyes welled up with tears. We can't contain this move of the Spirit in the meetings. It's already spilling over into the world.

Some christians struggle when you even mention the word, 'evangelism'. But what is evangelism really? Life — Jesus' life overflowing from us to others. Believers experience new things from God and tell their friends about it. Their friends then come to the meetings and are converted and baptised in the Spirit. Those who don't have much church background think that what we've got is normal christianity — and we're not going to tell them any different!

### The power to move in signs and wonders

After Jesus quoted Isaiah 61, He added, 'Today, this scripture is fulfilled in your hearing' (Luke 4:21). He was talking about

His performing signs and wonders among the people. Now I pray for individuals and watch as the Spirit comes on them, but to be honest, there aren't many signs and wonders. What I'm seeing is like a spray before the waterfall pours down.

Some people say, 'We've probably had enough now. Let's move on to something else.' Please, no! We haven't even begun. The Spirit gives us the power to move in signs and wonders. He wants miracles to become the norm — just as it was in Jesus' time and in the Acts of the apostles. The early church were moving in power and we have the same anointing as they did. The miracles that they saw, we should expect to see, and the same power that authenticated their ministry needs to authenticate ours as well.

After Peter and John were persecuted for healing a cripple, they met with other believers to pray. We read, 'they raised their voices together in prayer to God ... "Now, Lord, consider their threats and enable your servants to speak your word with great boldness. Stretch out your hand to heal and perform miraculous signs and wonders through the name of your holy servant Jesus." After they prayed, the place where they were meeting was shaken. And they were all filled with the Holy Spirit and spoke the word of God boldly' (Acts 4:24,29–31). The writer to the Hebrews says that God testified to the salvation message 'by signs, wonders and various miracles, and gifts of the Holy Spirit distributed according to his will' (Heb. 2:4).

It's the same Holy Spirit today, so surely it's still God's intention to testify to the salvation message by the same miraculous means. I look at our churches and nation and think,

'Lord, how desperately we need to see a demonstration of the power of your Spirit!' I praise Him for all His blessings, but I want to see this river deepening to include signs, wonders and miracles — not for our glory, so that we can gloat over what's happening among us, but for the praise and glory of His name.

The New Testament people were powerful. 'With great power the apostles continued to testify to the resurrection of the Lord Jesus, and much grace was upon them all' (Acts 4:33). 'The apostles performed many miraculous signs and wonders among the people' (Acts 5:12). 'People brought the sick into the streets and laid them on beds and mats so that at least Peter's shadow might fall on some of them as he passed by. Crowds gathered also from the towns around Jerusalem, bringing their sick and those tormented by evil spirits, and all of them were healed' (Acts 5:15,16). Paul said, 'The things that mark an apostle — signs, wonders and miracles — were done among you with great perseverance' (2 Cor. 12:12).

We're an apostolic people. We've been sent into the world not just to preach the Word and care for people, but also to confirm our message with signs and wonders. Some evangelists have tended to ignore the miraculous side of the gospel, but many of us know that it should be there and want to get into it. Maybe we're a bit fearful of it at first and wonder if we can handle it. Then we think, 'Hang on, the nations need this power encounter'. Then we link hands with other churches around the world and declare, 'Lord, You've been building us solidly on Your Word and we're secure in that. Now we're asking You for miracles. Make this movement of the Spirit mightier than anything we've ever known before.'

They're seeing this great power in China today. A Chinese pastor wrote the following astonishing account about the revival that's happening there.

'During these few years we have seen God move in a mighty way in China. Every place we go, we hear good news. The churches everywhere are experiencing great revival. People are being saved daily. In many places there are churches in every village and believers in every family. It excites us to hear these reports. As you know, these several years the Lord has moved on tens of thousands of His children, people of an excellent spirit who are willing to pay any price to serve Him, which is also a reason for this great revival.

'They've had a gospel month, and from the beginning to the end we experienced God's presence. In a period of a little over fifty days, there were 120,000 confirmed conversions to Christ in Henan province alone. This is God's own work for God works with us confirming the word with signs and wonders. Without these miracles, man alone would not be able to accomplish anything.

'Three sisters went to one district in Henan to evangelise, and after seven days of ministry, 1,100 people repented and were saved. It was as if there were fire in their hands, for whoever they laid their hands on, they immediately experienced a burning sensation all throughout their body and mighty power was released through their hands. In previous years when missionaries worked here, they didn't see such numbers converted, even after several dozen years. We sense now that this is the time for the Holy Spirit to mightily work through us.

'This is the Word the Lord said to Peter, "Launch out into the deep and let down your nets". Peter said, "At your word I will let down the nets". When he did so he enclosed a great multitude of fishes. As these three sisters were evangelising, a Gentile came forth and began to curse them without ceasing. However, they paid no attention to him, and after a long time other Gentiles came to the sisters and said, "Why is it that he has continually been cursing you and you have ignored him? In fact, you have shown compassion towards this man." As soon as they said that one sentence, this man suddenly collapsed on to the ground and died. It caused great awe and reverence toward the Lord in the crowd of people who witnessed this judgement of God. Thus many repented and accepted Jesus.

'There are many difficulties in open air street evangelism. However, through Chinese festivals, it is easier to go out into the open to preach the gospel. A whole group of people were thus preaching when PSB (Public Security Bureau) officials suddenly appeared. One of them stretched out his hand toward the sisters and shouted, "Arrest them". However, immediately his arm turned stiff in its stretched out position and he was not able to put it down or retract it. He went back to the PSB station in that condition and in desperation asked, "What can I do?" Someone said, "You must find some christians to pray for you". Therefore they invited our preachers to the PSB station to pray for him and when they did, he was healed. Then they preached to the police and many of them accepted the Lord.

'In another district a brother was gifted with a gift of healing and in the gospel month alone he healed 26 deaf people. Another man who was born with severe mental deficiency was considered an idiot. He was really dumb but after prayer his faculties were completely restored. In fact, God gave him a brilliant mind, excellent speech, talents and the ability to express himself so that everyone was amazed. He was previously considered a very stupid man and after this amazing healing, 83 people believed in the Lord.

'Previously, during our open air meetings, few people would pay any attention. Now everywhere when we go out with our tambourines and other instruments to praise and share Jesus, crowds of people stop everything they are doing to attend our meetings. As we preach, many cry out, "We have never heard such good news in all our lives. Why is it that no one has told us this good news before?" The people forget about all their plans and activities and remain for hours to listen to the gospel. It is truly the fire of the Holy Spirit burning in our midst.'

# Give it away

████████████ DAVID HOLDEN

We're living in amazing days. The Spirit is touching church after church and setting them ablaze. Now it's my conviction that where the Spirit is working powerfully, we need to know how to keep up the momentum, because we can't just stay where we are. We need to receive even more from God and I want to suggest how we can do that.

Before Jesus sent out His disciples, He told them, 'As you go, preach this message: "The kingdom of heaven is near." Heal the sick, raise the dead, cleanse those who have leprosy, drive out demons. Freely you have received, freely give' (Matt. 10:7,8). I think that this is a fun passage. When people in the church in Sidcup tell me, 'I really don't know what to do in this church,' I sometimes reply, 'Well, let's start here, shall we? Heal the sick, raise the dead, cleanse those with leprosy, drive out demons. When you've done that, come back and talk to me!'

The principle is this, 'Freely you have received, freely give.' We didn't buy or earn salvation, eternal life, or spiritual gifts.

They were freely given to us. The same is true of this fresh outpouring of the Holy Spirit. We don't receive a deeper touch from God because we're worthier than others. We receive because God loves us and wants to pour His blessings into our lives. Since He has given liberally to us, we should be liberal towards others. We don't say, 'Lord, please give me more of Your Spirit' merely because we want to be blessed, but because we want to bless other christians and a world that knows nothing of God's mercy and grace.

Jesus said, 'Give, and it will be given to you. A good measure, pressed down, shaken together and running over, will be poured into your lap. For with the measure you use, it will be measured to you' (Luke 6:38). The principle here is that if we give, it will be given to us. We should be people who declare, 'I don't want to become stale, so I'm going to give out as much as I can. Then God will pour more into my lap and I'll have more to give to others.' George Muller lived by this principle. He looked after thousands of orphans in Bristol in the last century but never publicised his need for financial help. He gave away from what little he had, and God kept on giving back to him. He soon discovered that he couldn't outgive God.

Again, Jesus said, 'From everyone who has been given much, much will be demanded; and from the one who has been entrusted with much, much more will be asked' (Luke 12:48). That's challenging. We receive a lot from God not so that we can say, 'I feel really blessed. What a great time I'm having!' God pours blessing into our lives because He wants blessing to pour out from our lives.

Plenty of oceans are swarming with life — that's because they've got rivers flowing in and out of them. The Dead Sea is different. It contains virtually no life because there's a river that flows in but nothing that flows out.

For every child of God there must be an outlet. However spectacular the blessing of God might be, unless that blessing results in giving away — sharing with others, allowing the life of God to overflow to a needy world — then it will eventually result in spiritual stagnation and malaise. We're not receiving so that we can be self-indulgent, but so that we can give away. That's the heart of God. Some people are asking, 'Why is God enriching and overwhelming us by His Spirit?' Surely, one of the reasons must be: He wants us to be so filled that we can't contain His blessing. It overflows the banks and touches everyone around us.

In parts of the country you can clearly see signs of past spiritual awakening — villages now full of empty chapels that were once filled with people overwhelmed by a fresh outpouring of the Holy Spirit. It didn't last. One reason for this is that a day came when the christians kept to themselves what God was giving to them. The outlet dried up.

We must learn from the mistakes of former generations. This move of the Spirit will continue and even increase if we're committed to giving away everything that God gives to us. Many people that I know are living by this principle and God is filling them more and more. Their attitude is, 'Lord, please can I receive from You — not because I'm selfish, but so I can bless others. I'd love to have the privilege of giving to them what you've given to me.'

God isn't reluctant to give. He doesn't splash small blessings on His people. Rather, He's a giving God who wants us to receive all that He has for us. Paul says that God 'did not spare his own Son, but gave him up for us all' (Rom. 8:32). Here's the ultimate expression of giving. If God has given us the most precious gift of all, then 'how will he not also, along with him, graciously give us all things?' The God who gave His Son wants to shower His blessing on us. This means that we've got to learn to receive. Once there's an inlet, there can be an outlet too.

We're rapidly learning that God wants us to receive again and again from Him. He wants to bless us abundantly. Many of us find this hard — mainly because we haven't fully grasped the grace of God. Jesus says, 'Ask, and it will be given to you' (Matt. 7:7). By faith we asked Jesus to forgive us and 'received the Spirit of sonship' (Rom. 8:15). Now we ask Him for more of the Spirit and receive that by faith too.

Speaking about communion, Paul said, 'I received from the Lord what I also passed on to you' (1 Cor. 11:23). He received something, then he imparted it. God wants us to be good receivers of the rain from heaven. It isn't cold English rain, the sort you try hard to avoid. It's warm rain in the desert, the sort you long to have pouring down your face. We're living in a wilderness — both inside and outside the church. The rain is just beginning to flood our lives and, like the desert, we need more and more.

Many of us will remember 1994 as a remarkable year, when God blessed us over and over again. It's hard to think of anything more wonderful than receiving. Jesus did. It's called giving. 'It is more blessed to give than to receive', He declared (Acts 20:35). Paul underlined the importance of giving when he commented, 'Whoever sows sparingly will also reap sparingly, and whoever sows generously will also reap generously' (2 Cor. 9:6). God didn't hold back, so neither should we. We should want to be generous because He is. The more we give, the more we will receive.

Jesus was baptised in water and in the Spirit. Then the Spirit strengthened Him in the wilderness. After forty days Jesus returned in the power of the Spirit and the first thing He did was give away. He read from Isaiah 61 — whose focus is entirely on giving out — and then went out and fulfilled it. He preached the good news, set captives free and healed the sick. Jesus was anointed by the Spirit to give away. He received from God, ministered to the people and returned to God to receive more. That's what we should be doing too.

God poured out His Spirit on the disciples on the day of Pentecost. It must have been a tremendous experience — wind, tongues of fire, new languages, drunkenness, an extraordinary sense of the presence of God. How tempting it might have been simply to bask in God's love! But what was the first thing the disciples did? They gave it away. They spilled out on to the streets and Peter told the onlookers, 'The promise is for you and your children and for all who are far off' (Acts 2:39). Those early christians knew that the coming of the Spirit wasn't just for them, but for others too. So no sooner had the Spirit come on them, than they moved into action and 3,000 people were added in one day.

If it's more blessed to give than to receive, then we need to start asking God how He wants His life to flow through us to others. We're all individuals, so God's plans for each of us will differ from those of others. Let me encourage you to jot down some ideas of the sort of ways in which you could bless those around you. If everyone in your local church did that and began to reach out to others, wonderful things would begin to happen. I'll give you five ideas of practical outlets that should result from receiving.

EXTRAVAGANT WORSHIP If you're grateful for God's love poured into your life, the most natural outlet will be adoration. To worship intimately is to acknowledge who God is and what He's done. To stop worshipping is the first step to over familiarity — abandoning your first love and taking your salvation for granted. Let's be extravagant worshippers. This new anointing must result in more love for Jesus. What counts isn't how you perform in public, but how your worship develops in private. Intimate worship should overflow into every day and become a lifestyle.

DYNAMIC PRAYER A touch from God will stir us to pray. Many of us are tired of 'going through the motions' in our prayer life. Paul felt like that and said, 'The Spirit helps us in our weakness. We do not know what we ought to pray for, but the Spirit himself intercedes for us' (Rom. 8:26). The key is to be filled with the Spirit and prayer is the outlet. We must learn to intercede in the Spirit. I know several people who are saying, 'I can't stop praying'. I wish I were one of them! They 'just don't know where the time went'. It won't always be like that, but oh for more dynamic and anointed prayer!

As our churches are affected by this time of refreshing, the result must be an increase in our corporate gatherings for prayer. I expect this move of God to result in a 'house of prayer' just as it was in Acts. As we receive together we should naturally want to pray together. This anointing isn't given primarily so that christians can enjoy themselves more, but so that they can cry out to God for a nation without hope.

JOYFUL SERVICE Spiritual manifestations are secondary to the fruit of changed lives. Change implies love which is expressed through joyful service. People will know that you've received a new touch from God when they see how you love others — not just in word, but in deed too. This will probably require time, energy, inconvenience and sacrifice.

With the exception of private tongues, we receive the gifts of the Spirit for the edification of others, not ourselves. Peter says, 'Each one should use whatever gift he has received to serve others' (1 Pet. 4:10). Here it is again: we receive to serve. If I ever pray for someone after a meeting, I try to get that person to pray for others. I find that they're usually the most effective at it because they've just received.

HILARIOUS GIVING There's a lot of laughter around, but who would link that with the offering? If God has been generous to us, it makes sense for us to be generous in return. Generous and joyful giving tends not to be a characteristic of the British church. The Bible frequently teaches about giving, but we don't like to talk about it, preferring to separate our finances into a 'secular department' rather than associate giving with the Spirit's anointing.

We got on to the subject of money at one of our Saturday morning prayer meetings. Someone had a prophetic word about there not being one area of our lives which we keep from the outpouring of the Spirit. God said, 'Anointed people become anointed givers. If you've been anointed by the Spirit, let your giving be anointed. Even your pockets are not hidden from Me.' Our response was hilarious. We all emptied our pockets and turned them inside out. Then we prayed, 'Lord, we're doing this to remind ourselves that there's nothing hidden from You'. We'd hardly finished praying than the Spirit just fell on us. Since then, many have testified that their view of giving has totally changed. Has the anointing of God penetrated every area of your life?

POWER EVANGELISM Let's face it, when all's said and done, this present move of the Spirit will fade unless it results in our reaching out to our neighbours and friends with renewed compassion and an increased desire to see them converted. When Jesus exhorted His disciples, 'Freely you have received, freely give,' He was probably thinking of their going out into the world. He told them, 'You will receive power when the Holy Spirit comes on you; and you will be my witnesses' (Acts 1:8). We don't need a new approach to evangelism. We need to receive a greater anointing of the Spirit so that we can become more effective in sharing our faith.

We can't contain what God is doing. It keeps spilling over. The pastor of a church went to the Airport Vineyard Church in Toronto and God really blessed him. While he was there he went on a boat near the Niagara Falls. He was so overwhelmed by the cascading water and the power of God that he hit the deck! The people on the boat were really concerned, but the friends who were with him just laughed and said, 'He's fine'! Then there was a wedding where people prayed for the bride and groom and they both crashed on to the floor — much to the bewilderment of unbelievers on both sides of the family. This sort of thing has even happened at baptisms!

God wants this blessing to flow over our lives and into the lives of others. Maybe you've been asking for more of the Spirit because you're keen to be blessed. Why not change your motivation a bit? Say to God, 'Lord, I want You to pour out Your abundant blessing on me because I want to bless others'. I've seen many people do that and they've received a fresh anointing from God.

So as the river of God continues to gather strength, make sure that there's an outlet. May there be plenty of giving away in your life. May doors open out of which the rivers of living water can flow. If He anoints your head with oil, make sure your cup is overflowing. Pray that God's people will receive more and more, but also that our giving will outweigh our receiving. If we're givers as well as receivers, then the river, far from being stagnant, will flood the nations with life. And what God has begun will continue towards its great goal when 'the earth will be full of the knowledge of the LORD as the waters cover the sea' (Isa. 11:9).

# What should leaders be thinking?

DAVID HOLDEN

People are really enjoying this outpouring of the Holy Spirit and God is touching them in remarkable ways. As I've travelled around, I've noted what's been happening in the churches and I'd like to help leaders to understand the season in which we're living so that they can sustain and even increase the blessing of God among their people.

## Take people further

When the Spirit first breaks out in a church, He comes like a match to wood. You're praying for individuals and suddenly, much to your surprise, things begin to happen. The Spirit lights a fire in people's hearts and it blazes for several weeks. Then everyone starts to become over familiar with the exhortation to 'come forward and receive a fresh touch from God'. The powerful experiences seem to die down and become the norm, and people begin to question, 'Why do I need to keep on being filled with the Holy Spirit?'

There are two issues here: the lighting of the fire and the fanning of the flame. Once the fire has been lit, you can't just keep on lighting it over and over again. In order to move on, you have to fan the flame. But how? By speaking the Word of God to your people. You give them Scriptural reasons why they need to be filled with the Spirit and they'll respond with greater receptivity than ever before — because the fire has already been lit and you're fanning it into flame.

Let me illustrate this. The lead elder of my local church at Sidcup once preached on the intimacy of our love for Jesus. He talked about the love that the Father had for His Son and exhorted us to love Jesus as God does. 'The only way you can do this is by revelation' he said. 'The Holy Spirit comes and gives us revelation about God's love. We need to be filled with the Holy Spirit so that we can love Jesus more.' When he made an appeal to come forward at the end of the meeting, people flocked forward. Why? Because they were saying to themselves, 'Yes, this is why I need to be filled with the Spirit again and again. It's because I want to love Jesus as the Father loves Him.'

So if the fire has been lit in your local church, don't just step back and say, 'Lord, do whatever You want to and we'll just sit back and enjoy it'. Get in there and start fanning it. You can't stay where you started in the early days, you must move on. It's the responsibility of leaders to bring content and to ensure that the flame is fanned into a mighty blaze.

## Be convinced that this is of God

These days people are likening this outpouring of the Spirit to the river in Ezekiel 47. You can paddle in this river, or swim in it. Now God doesn't want His people to be content with an ankle deep experience of the Spirit, He wants us to be drenched. So why do some churches seem to be saturated, while others remain in the shallows? I think that the main reason lies in leadership. If a church is being overwhelmed, it's because the leaders are being overwhelmed. If the church is being largely unaffected, I immediately start asking questions about its leaders.

The key is this: leaders must be convinced that this move of the Spirit is from God. God said to Ezekiel, 'Son of man, do you see this?' (Ezek. 47:6) Now Ezekiel had done more than see the river, he'd actually touched it. But God still asked the question. The meaning behind it wasn't just, 'Do you see?' but 'Do you perceive?' In other words, 'Where does this river come from? Is it from God, or is it just man's idea?' If you're convinced, 'Yes, this is a sovereign move of God,' then the question still comes back to you, 'Do you see it? Do you see how much your church really needs this move of the Spirit?' Once you're convinced that God is behind it, you'll go for it with all your might. You'll know that the Spirit won't harm your people, but that He'll bring them into more and more blessing.

Leaders have a tremendous responsibility because they can either usher people into the blessing of God or keep them from it. Some leaders are holding their congregations back from all that God has for them because they're trying to tack this move of the Spirit on to what they're already doing. 'We'll pray for people in the corner at the end of the Sunday morning meeting' they say. But that's a very crossable river. If you let the river flow, you'll be so open to God that you'll allow Him to come in and move on you anytime. You can't carry on as you were before. God wants every area of church life to be transformed by the Spirit. So you need to be convinced that it's of God and be focused.

I thank God that my elders keep encouraging me to stay focused. I'm always getting up and talking about the blessing of God. The church members probably sit there thinking, 'Why does this guy go on and on and on?' The reason is this: I have a conviction, and the conviction is that this move of the Spirit isn't just for a few of God's people, but for all of them. I'll carry on talking about the Spirit while God lights fires in their lives and I'll go on fanning into flame all that He's doing.

You need to guard against being distracted from what God is doing. You can't look out at a sea of faces on Sunday morning and think, 'I don't think we'll leave room for anything extraordinary today because the people don't look too keen'. If you decide what God wants to do on the basis of how the members look, you won't do much. You must have the conviction, 'Yes, this is a move of God. My church needs this blessing. I'm not going to tack it on. Rather, I'm going to keep myself focused and be open for God to do anything He wants.'

## Lead by example

Many leaders ask, 'In the meetings, do I stand back and comment objectively on what's happening and miss out myself? Or do I get so filled with the Spirit that I'm almost incapable of doing much about what's going on?' Well, leaders have the responsibility of teaching and caring for people, but if they remain objective commentators and fail to drink from the river themselves, they'll start to dry up.

They can't afford to be passive observers; they must be enthusiastic participators.

At Sidcup we believe that God wants to impart to us leaders so that we can bless His people. That's why we're at the forefront of this move of the Spirit. At least one of us will stay 'sober' — because that gives security to the congregation. But the rest of us just plunge in. The church takes its cue from us. People are thrilled to bits when they see us receiving the Spirit and staggering round almost incapable of doing anything — and enjoying every minute.

The best way of leading your people into this move of the Spirit is through personal experience — you get into the river and start swimming. You can't impart much to others if you're just paddling around yourself. But if you're overwhelmed by the presence of God and drenched in the Spirit, then you won't be commentating on what's happening. You'll be giving out to others from what God has given to you.

One mark of this new move of God is that people need to receive again and again — which is a strange idea for those who've been baptised in the Spirit for many years. If this continual receiving is necessary for the ordinary members, how much more should it be true for leaders? Sometimes elders I meet tell me, 'Not much is happening in our church at the moment'. Immediately, I'm asking, 'What about you guys? When you have your leaders' meetings, are you laying hands on each other and praying for one another?' Many of them reply, 'No. We just talk about church matters'. It really amazes me because what happens among the leaders is a major key to what happens in the rest of the church. In our elders' meetings we're always praying for each other and falling around laughing. Other things have gone by the board. But I have the sneaking suspicion that we're better at leading the church now than we ever were when we were discussing the items on our agenda.

I travel round a lot, so people are often praying for me. I minister at a meeting or conference and at the end, a few individuals will come up to me and say, 'Can we pray for you, please?' I readily agree because I've been giving out and want to receive. Our ministry team have really grasped hold of this giving and receiving thing. If they've been praying for others, they're not allowed to go home until they've been prayed for. It's hilarious! By the end of the meeting they're really moving in the power of the Spirit, and are all over the floor. It's a question of, 'last one up, pray for yourself!'

That's the attitude we should be having as leaders. Those of us who've come from evangelical backgrounds will remember the days when the deacons processed single file into the Sunday meeting place. Now things are a bit different — the leaders are being carried in! If you really believe that this is all of God, you must put a high priority on ministering to each other. The ministry of the Holy Spirit will flow out from your leaders' meetings and into the church.

### Change the wineskin
God is giving us new wine, so it's got to affect the wineskin. In other words, you can't just go on as you were before. You must say, 'Lord, You have Your agenda. Everything's open to You. We want Your Spirit to be in control.' For example, if before the Spirit hit the church you'd planned a series of guest

services, you must do some radical thinking because God might not want you to continue with them.

This doesn't mean that you neglect preaching the Word or other foundational values— although you may have to allow them to take on a different shape, and even increase as a result of what's happening. The most important thing is this: that you provide an opportunity for people to drink. That may be on Sunday nights or at the prayer meetings. You may even decide to close down all your housegroups for a season and come together on a weeknight to receive.

I don't fully understand why we've got to keep on receiving, but it's clear that the more you allow people to pray for you, the more you're filled with the Spirit. So if your structure doesn't allow this to happen, your people will dry up and so too will the move of the Spirit. If you want the Spirit to continue to break into church life, you must look hard at your church structures and release individuals to minister to each other.

Perhaps one of the dangers is that the Sunday morning meetings end up by being less lively than the Sunday night meetings — because in the morning people are thinking about lunch and collecting their children. I don't have all the answers, but I do feel that whatever's happening on Sunday mornings should be touched by this move of God. Wives with young children or non-christian husbands may not be able to get to other meetings during the week and they need to receive from God just as much as everyone else. There won't be time for hours of ministry to one another, but the worship should be fresh and the preaching powerfully anointed by the Spirit. If I come to your church on a Sunday morning, I should sense from the worship and preaching whether the Holy Spirit is affecting everything that's going on.

Every part of our church life must be touched by this move of the Spirit. It can't go on as it was before. I know churches where worship leaders and musicians have had to stop leading worship so that they could receive from God. And children's workers have said, 'I don't think I can do children's work any more. It wasn't a problem when I was teaching about Noah. But now, when the children are all lying on the floor meeting with God, I don't know what to do.' Is the Spirit affecting your wineskin? How much have you allowed the river to flow into every part of church life?

## Don't feel guilty

Many people are asking, 'Where's this move of the Spirit going?' The answer is simple, 'Out!' If it's not going out into the world, it will fade away. That's why we don't have to go round feeling guilty that we're enjoying what God is doing now. He started it and if He wants us to receive a lot so that we can give a lot, who are we to worry? If we all closed down now because we were worried about where this thing was going, we probably wouldn't have much to give when we got there. So I refuse to feel guilty that I'm not praying for revival every moment of the day. I just want to enjoy the fullness of what God has for me, and when it goes forward, so will I.

When people say to me, 'Do you think this thing's peaking?' I reply, 'Yes. I hope so, because I think there are higher peaks that we've yet to reach'. They don't expect that answer. They think that once you hit a peak it's downhill from then on. Some of them say, 'I think I've received enough from God'. I answer, 'Enough to change the world?' And they say, 'No, I don't think so'. There's a lot more receiving that needs to go on. In fact, we've hardly even started!

## Maintain spontaneity

It's remarkable how quickly we build traditions into the way we do things. Some of these are helpful in that they provide an opportunity for more to happen, but when they become rigid, they stifle spontaneity. We can't say, 'We know how the Spirit operates now'. We don't know anything really. Tomorrow is a new day and we can't be sure what's going to happen in it. We must maintain spontaneity.

A major key to great spontaneity — particularly on Sunday mornings — is this: before the meeting starts, pray for the worship leader and the person who's going to speak. I used to think that prayer before the meeting was just a routine thing we used to do — 'God bless this person and that'. Now it's totally different. The prayer meeting may be only ten minutes long, but I want to be there to drink and minister. When we pray for one of our worship leaders, he often gets up on the platform, clings to the pulpit, shakes and struggles to speak. If people are a bit dry, people just look at him and think, 'Oh, we're in the presence of God' and suddenly there's spontaneity. They don't know what's going to happen and there's an openness to what God wants to do.

This move of the Spirit will restore spontaneity to our churches and we must resist the temptation to fall back into predictability. What was overwhelmingly fresh a few weeks ago can so quickly become familiar. 'This week we had a tongue, an interpretation, a prophecy, a word of knowledge, three people laughed and two fell down. It wasn't a bad time.' We used to say, 'The singing in the Spirit was pretty good'. Now it's, 'Three laughed and two fell down. There weren't many phenomena this morning.' Phenomena aren't the issue. The issue is this: 'Was the presence of God there?' We mustn't lose the awe of what's happening.

Whenever I pray for someone and something happens, I don't want to think, 'Oh yes, she's shaking again and will probably fall over in a minute'. I want to think, 'I'm not doing this, Lord. You're breaking in. You're blessing her. It's terrific.' My eyes have got to be open to what's really happening. Even people who don't like what's going on will get over familiar with it all, and in the end they'll accommodate it. 'Three laugh and two fall down' — they'll add that in, but won't see what God is doing. There must be room for spontaneity. I just love getting into gatherings where you know that the people are open to the spontaneous move of the Spirit.

You'll really need to think hard about your worship leaders, particularly those who think, 'This is my part of the meeting.' These days, the preachers are wondering if they're going to preach, so why shouldn't the worship leaders question whether they're going to lead worship? Some of them are amazingly sensitive to this move of the Spirit. They don't have a great list of songs that they've got to get through. Rather, they start with a couple of ideas and see what happens. Worship leaders aren't there to entertain, but to lead people into the presence of God. Certainly, if nothing much seems to be happening, they need to question, 'Shall we go on or stop?' It's a matter of spontaneity, not of losing one's brain. And if you think certain worship leaders are hindering the work of the Spirit, get up on the platform and pray for them so that God can move freely again!

At one of our elders' meetings there was a prophetic word which said, 'Walk among the people.' We knew that some individuals were rather nervous about coming to the front for prayer and sensed that God was telling us to start moving among them. So in our meetings we began walking around, looking for what God was doing and praying for individuals where they were — if they wanted us to do that, of course. We don't want this to become a formula, but neither do we want everything to be happening at the front.

## Maintain your values

While you need to maintain your values, you must allow them to be touched afresh by this new move of the Spirit. You don't say, 'Good relationships and accountability aren't that relevant any more'. Nor do you neglect preaching the word. These things are vital. You still want to welcome your guests too. You don't want non-christians coming in sheepishly while your people are all 'going for it' and totally ignoring them.

Several people have said to me, 'There are a lot of evangelicals coming to our meetings and they haven't been baptised in the Spirit. But God is moving on them. What do you think about that?' I think that we present the truth to them. If an unbeliever comes into our meeting and is overpowered by God, we encourage him to go on a 'Just Looking' course where we can explain that Jesus has met with them powerfully.

Similarly, if a non-charismatic falls over in a meeting, we don't assume, 'Oh, you're baptised in the Spirit now' because we might be robbing him of the real thing. He'll go home thinking that he's received something that he hasn't. No, we talk to him about the doctrine of the baptism in the Spirit. He may have been closed to it once, but now that God has met with him, he'll probably be far more willing to listen.

In one meeting, some people prayed for my youngest daughter, Julia, who was seven. She fell on the floor and lay there angelic, her little hands waving around. The christians who were praying for her knew that she hadn't been baptised in the Spirit, so when she got up, they asked her if she wanted this experience. She said she did — there was an immediate receptivity. She was filled with the Spirit and spoke in tongues. I'm glad those people did that. She could have gone home having fallen over in a meeting — a very real, valid experience. But she came away with far more because we remained true to our values.

### Enjoy the unity of the Spirit

Some churches may well be criticising the current move of the Spirit, but in the main, there's a wonderful sense of goodwill, fellowship, love and unity right across all the denominations. Paul says, 'Make every effort to keep the unity of the Spirit' (Eph. 4:3). We're not coming together on the basis of our doctrines, but on this move of the Spirit because it's hit everybody.

Not too long ago I was invited to address a large gathering of leaders in Westminster Central Hall. The people there were from many different streams across London and Roger Forster was leading the meeting. Once I wouldn't have been invited into such a setting, but this move of the Spirit broke down the barriers and we had a great time. At one point, a number of us on the platform were holding hands and singing a new song and the presence of God was awesome. After the meeting people just kept on coming up to me and saying, 'We're so thrilled to see you. It's wonderful that you're here.'

This blessing of the Spirit isn't just for certain churches, it's for all God's people. You must be generous hearted and give away what He's giving to you. Sometimes you'll find yourself in funny and even awkward situations — particularly when you're dealing with people who don't agree with you on certain things. You'll have to hold on to biblical values, but you needn't stop enjoying the unity and having a heart for the wider body of Christ.

## Glorifying to Jesus

You must check things out. Some people say and do things that don't glorify Jesus. You don't need a word of knowledge or a gift of discernment to reveal that. You just need to get in there and say gently, 'That wasn't quite right.' Powerful things are happening in the meetings and you must watch your motives closely. If you don't, you might start thinking that your church is something special and start glorifying it. I believe that God wants to see a move of the Spirit which isn't characterised by famous people and we must ensure that this is the way it is.

There will often be a queue of people who want you, and you only, to pray for them and you've got to watch it. Certainly, some christians are more gifted than others at imparting blessing and you need to recognise who they are. But you must remember that people will flock not just to you, but to the anointing that is upon you. The glory must always go to Jesus. It's simple to spot whether an individual is glorifying Jesus. You look for the fruit of the Spirit. Does this person really love Jesus? Is he or she bringing the presence and power of God into situations? Is the heart motive pure? These are the things that are really important.

# How should leaders
# be responding?

TERRY VIRGO

For decades I've been longing for revival. Great men like Arthur Wallis have taught me to pray fervently for it and to expect God to move in power. Early in 1994 if anyone had pointed to the things that have been happening in the church and said to me 'This is how revival is going to begin,' I'd have been very surprised. I feel that we've been overtaken by something quite extraordinary, but very welcome. I value this move of the Holy Spirit because it's bearing positive fruit in the lives of those who are being touched by it.

## People are experiencing God's presence

This is the first thing that I notice: people are aware of the presence of God in a new way. Many people know that they've been saved and baptised in the Holy Spirit, but have had a largely intellectual approach to their faith. They've been ticking over, perhaps exercising spiritual gifts, but they've grown somewhat stale. Then God has broken in and suddenly they're testifying that, 'He feels so close. It's wonderful.'

### People are experiencing God's love

We know that God communicates His love through His Word and in the way that He orders our steps. It's one thing to know that in our heads, but it's a very different thing when God hits us with His love. On the day of Pentecost the crowd thought that the disciples were drunk, and it's this sense of drunkenness that people are experiencing in this current move of the Spirit. They're no longer reasoning, 'Yes, Jesus loves me, the Bible tells me so'. They're saying, 'I know that He loves me because I can hardly bear the intensity of it'.

I prayed for a man who fell over and cried and cried. I sensed that God wanted me to tell him, 'You're precious to Me. My family would be incomplete without you. You're so valued.' Suddenly his weeping turned to laughter. He was rolling around, completely drunk in the Spirit, overwhelmed by the love of God. That's so much more wonderful than telling someone, 'Just read this verse and believe what it says'. There's nothing like the immediate activity of God — particularly when He's saying how much He loves you.

### People are experiencing God's power

Sometimes our christianity can drift into little more than good works. Christians think, 'I need to be serving God' but that becomes almost the sum total of why they're here. Then God's Spirit sweeps in and overwhelms them. They sense His power and immediately want to lay hands on others so that they can receive from God too.

### How are people responding to this outpouring?

When I first started going to meetings where the Spirit was moving among the people, I really wasn't impressed. In fact,

I was quite surprised by what was happening. I couldn't understand the value of people shaking and falling down. But then I heard the testimonies. People were saying that their marriages had been restored and their attitudes changed. That, for me, was far more impressive. As the Spirit works in people's lives, they begin to respond in new ways.

PRAYER Many churches have discovered that there's a greater focus on prayer. Numbers at regular prayer meetings have increased, people want to pray for longer than the set time and are more fervent than ever before. In addition, prayer meetings are springing up all over the place. Young people who used to say, 'Let's watch a video' are now saying, 'Come round and pray'. The Spirit is moving on them and they're receiving amazing revelations from God. Individuals too have been gripped by a new urgency to pray and are spending long periods of time crying out to God for breakthrough in their personal situations and in their town and nation.

INVOLVEMENT People who used to be on the edge of things want to be in the centre. One man stood up in front of the church and said, 'I was only coming along to give my tithe. I was always at the back and when the meeting finished, I was out. But one day one of you guys prayed for me and the Spirit came on me. Then someone asked me to pray for someone else. Well I was barely coming along, let alone praying for others. But I went up to this man, closed my eyes and prayed for him. When I opened my eyes he was on the floor!' No longer does that guy think, 'Here we go again, another meeting'. He's been transformed. God has given him a new appetite for His house and he wants to be at everything that's going.

RELATIONSHIPS A church leader wrote to me to say that he'd never seen so many broken relationships restored. People have written to him to say that they've settled old scores and want to be right both with God and with others.

WITNESS People want to share their faith — as individuals and in groups. There's an added dynamic in their witness too. One woman was visited by a door to door book salesman. She invited him in and he was overwhelmed by the presence of God.

BODY LIFE When churches were small, there was quite a lot of participation in the meetings. But as we've grown there's been a decline in the manifestation of spiritual gifts and a greater emphasis on platform led ministry. Since this current move of the Spirit there's been a new desire to be involved — not just in the main meetings, but also in small groups. People no longer want to be listeners alone. They want to be the channels of God's love to others. So they're going up to one another before they go home on Sundays and saying, 'Can I pray for you?' It's great.

PROPHECY I've discovered that when leaders meet they've been giving prophecies of far greater revelation and authority than ever before. I believe that as leaders continue to spend time together, there will be an increase in the depth of prophecy. This will be true of our regular meetings too. A little while ago a woman who wouldn't be regarded as particularly strong spiritually, fell on the floor at a prayer meeting and gave an extraordinarily powerful prophecy — full of doctrine and truth which was way beyond her experience.

These responses aren't just the results of a fad. It's an authentic move from God — but we mustn't overstate it. Although we're seeing some conversions, people aren't yet flocking to Jesus or salvation. Similarly, there are some healings, but not many yet. I've been surprised that there haven't been more healings and want to urge people to, 'call on (God) while he is near' (Isa. 55:6). We also need to pray for a greater impartation of the Spirit — not just directly from God, but through one another too.

I'm amazed at the power in people's ministries today. It's phenomenal. God is blessing so many people and I hesitate to say, 'I don't quite agree with that'. However, I feel that I must be true to the Scriptures and there are some things that I can't go along with. I don't want to rubbish what's going on but I can't take on board everything that's happening.

God tends to work through two channels: power and teaching. Unquestionably, Samson had power from God, but his lifestyle was way out of line. If we saw a modern christian like him, we'd say, 'Look at this guy's life. His power can't be from God.' Samson was an unsanctified man, but his power was most definitely from God. Power isn't a reward for sanctification. You can pray, 'Oh, Lord, make me more holy so that I can have more power', but power is more a gift of grace than of merit. In the end, God had to judge Samson. His sin found him out and he reaped what he'd sown.

It's easy to think, 'God has powerfully anointed this man. Everything he says must be theologically right.' But that's not necessarily true. The truth is in the Bible and we must keep coming back to it. We must be careful in the way we interpret it too. It's easy to pick up tradition without realising what we're doing. So let's not speak against people who are moving in power, but let's not throw away our Bibles either. God wants us to worship Him 'in spirit and truth' (John 4:23). Let's do that.

## How should leaders respond to this outpouring?

GIVE A CLEAR LEAD If we're leaders, we need to consider what's happening and battle through our own reservations. Only then can we lead our people with confidence and peace. We mustn't just talk about things in a casual way or sow seeds of caution. Rather, we must honour what God is doing and speak confidently about it. If people see us doing that, they'll find security in our leadership.

GIVE PERSONAL TESTIMONY People gather to our leadership gifts, and it will help them if we can share our own personal experience and confidence in what God is doing. Let's use the testimonies of others too. Maybe after the preaching we could read out a letter, or invite a couple of individuals to the front to explain what happened to them and how they felt about it. People identify with that so well. They think, 'That person is just like me. I was wondering what was happening to him while he was lying on the floor. Now I understand.'

It also helps people to hear that other churches, and nations, are experiencing the same things. Sometimes individuals can think, 'We're getting isolated from other churches. Maybe this thing is getting a bit "cult-like"' and that idea can make them afraid. But if we teach them that this move of the Spirit is widespread, they'll be much happier about it.

We must encourage people to look at church history too. Although some books have been written by sceptics, there are many well-researched books which illustrate the way in which God has moved in power during times of revival. Charles Finney and Jonathan Edwards were mightily touched by the Spirit of God. There were also some extraordinary manifestations in the Salvation Army. We tend to associate them with their splendid social activities, but their origins are in amazing power. Let's help our people through testimony.

TEACH THE WORD INTO IT It's easy to think, 'We're in this now. We'll just let it ride.' We must keep bringing the Word of God into it. How do we respond when people say, 'This isn't being done in a fitting and orderly way'? (1 Cor. 14:40) Well, Martyn Lloyd-Jones once pointed out that Paul was speaking into the context of incredible life. Believers were falling over each other to prophesy, babbling away in tongues and behaving inappropriately during the Lord's Supper. Paul was challenging them about their lack of restraint and encouraging them to get some sort of order into what they were doing. If he were here today, he wouldn't be responding in the same way. He'd probably wander into a few church buildings and puzzle why the congregations were so lifeless. We need to embrace order, but not sit in death.

Sometimes people bring their own human disposition and project it back on to God. 'God is a gentleman,' they say. 'I don't think God is like that. He wouldn't do things that way.' I once saw a man fall on the floor. His wife turned to someone standing nearby and said, 'Do you think that Jesus would do that?' And the reply was, 'I think He just did.' We must submit to God as He's revealed in the Word and not to our own ideas of what He's like or what He can or can't do.

When David escaped from Saul and went to Naioth, Saul sent three detachments of soldiers after him and each detachment ended up prophesying. Then Saul himself went to Naioth, but before he even arrived, the Spirit of God came on him and he too prophesied. None of these men volunteered to prophesy. The Spirit overcame them (1 Sam. 19:18–24). We can't say, 'God never overrides our will. He wouldn't do unexpected things.' We mustn't try to make everything ordinary — because we're living in an extraordinary season. Let's show people that what's happening is thoroughly biblical and be open to everything that God wants to do among us.

MAKE SPACE One church leader said to his congregation, 'For the next three months, anything goes!' It sounds crazy really! But what he was saying was, 'Let's make lots of space for what God's doing.' We mustn't assume that we've got to have every ingredient in every meeting. Years ago if I went to a meeting and there was no preaching, I'd think, 'This church is unbalanced'. Now I think that there are times when we skip the preaching to focus on something else. I'm not saying, 'Let's not bother with Bible teaching any more'. I'm saying, 'Let's recognise the seasons'. The early believers 'devoted themselves to the apostles' teaching and to the fellowship, to the breaking of bread and to prayer' (Acts 2:42). Such structures never change, but they can be shaped by the Spirit.

We must give people enough space to make mistakes. Sometimes I'm sitting in meetings and the person ministering has let something go which I would have pounced on. 'Come

Holy Spirit,' they say, and immediately all kinds of stuff begins to happen. I'm thinking, 'Why don't you stop that?' but they let it ride and maybe give a brief explanation. I admire that. What they're really doing is letting people find their own way through. They know that if they correct things too quickly, those who aren't prone to going over the top will back down and never risk anything.

One man said to his congregation, 'I'd rather have one prophecy in a year which is authentically from God than a whole load that aren't'. That's so unhelpful. God operates through weak believers who are often fearful of being wrong. If they hear us making a big deal of getting it right, then they'll go into their holes and say, 'OK, you do it. We're just feeble saints. You obviously know what you're doing. So you get on with it.' We've got to keep building a foundation of love and be patient with people. Certainly, we'll make many mistakes, but we still need to get right into what God is doing.

God once spoke to a group of leaders about this. One of the guys there saw a picture of some cement being laid and setting. When the rain began to fall, someone was tempted to go off and get a tarpaulin to protect the cement. But God intervened. He was saying, 'Don't do that. The cement is well set. I gave you water to lay it. Now I'm giving you a new kind of water. So don't be afraid and cover it all up. The foundations are well laid. Expose them to the flood.' If we haven't worked hard at laying good doctrine in our churches, then we've got problems. But if we have, then we can risk the flood.

Another picture came to someone else in another meeting. It was like a TV advertisement for a car. The car was under a large sheet and you could see its magnificent shape and smooth aerodynamic form. Then the sheet was taken away and the vehicle under it was an agricultural machine bristling with blades and sharp ragged edges. God said to the group, 'You like it to look good. I'm trying to get a job done and you're trying to make it look smooth. Please loosen up.' God is about a great work and if we're too refined, He'll mess us up. He wants to use sharp threshing instruments having teeth, not the smoothest, latest machines. Let's make space for Him.

I shared a prophetic word at a church prayer meeting about our being in white water. We'd been coming along a smooth river and suddenly we'd hit this white water with all its dangers, turmoil, pain, disappointment and bewilderment. Someone there, a Canadian, said that he'd been in this sort of environment. He recalled an occasion when he and some friends were in canoes and described what it felt like to ride on white water. He said, 'It was so exciting that after we'd gone through it all, we got out of the river, picked up the canoes and did it over again. The third time we abandoned the canoes altogether, jumped into the water with our lifejackets on, and just let the water carry us along. It was so exhilarating.' Riding the waves takes skill. You've got to move with the water. We've got to learn how to be less rigid and move with God.

It's tempting to look around and think, 'God seems to be using others far more than me in this move of the Spirit'. Whereas once we felt comfortable in our training, gifting and position, suddenly we're not so sure of ourselves. We see some guy moving with great power and think, 'Wow! Look what happens when he prays for people. I feel so vulnerable.' We must make space for gifted individuals, but we mustn't hand them the reins of our spiritual leadership or our people will begin to feel insecure. We mustn't clamp down or throw away. Rather, we must continue to fulfil our calling as leaders and bring maturity into the church.

In May 1994 I was at a conference. We'd planned to have several teaching sessions, but God came so powerfully in some of these that we changed our plans. God blitzed one session, so we just spent the time praying for each other. We directed the next meeting more and invited all the senior pastors to the front where we prayed for them. God came powerfully on them and they received many prophetic words. We could have abandoned the preaching in the final session, but I felt strongly that I was meant to speak. As I did so, a few people began to crack up and laugh, but I still pressed on. Those who couldn't contain themselves ran out or somehow stifled their joy. Several individuals came up to me afterwards and said, 'Thank you so much. We needed that word.' We've got to be sensitive and learn how to handle these things.

These things can sound very scary, but we've got to learn how to respond to them. Sometimes God will sweep in and there's nothing you can do. On other occasions, you can channel what's happening or you can carry on with your original programme — even though people are running for the door. A guy who was ministering at a large meeting was conscious that the Holy Spirit was breaking out in one particular place. Rather than let things go he said, 'The Spirit isn't moving across the whole room, but God is really blessing that little group. There's a room just across the corridor. Go and enjoy God.' And with that, he carried on with the meeting. When the Spirit began to move at the end of the meeting he said, 'Get those others back in.'

Let's not become weird. You may be praying with someone, nothing much seems to be happening and you're questioning, 'What's going on? I'm a leader here so I'm supposed to know what to do. So what am I supposed to do?' Suddenly you're feeling that everything is out of your control and you're scared. Fear is a powerful weapon of the enemy, but you mustn't yield to it. Remember the years of faithful service that you've put in and the trust that people have in you. Say to the person you're praying for, 'Is God saying anything to you?' Take responsibility.

## What should leaders watch out for?

THE DISAPPOINTED Some people feel untouched and are bewildered because nothing seems to be happening to them. They feel like the boulders in the white water — hit by the enemy with words like, 'God doesn't love you. He's touching everyone else, but you're excluded.' These people can become so discouraged that they withdraw to the edges. We must minister the love of God to them and encourage them — both personally and in our housegroup meetings.

PRETENDED SIGNS People can do things which aren't Spirit led. Maybe we pray for them and they fall over just to please us. But they get up thinking, 'There's nothing in this'. Then they become cynical, switch off and drift away. Unreality isn't always easy to discern, but we must gently challenge it and draw out the truth.

A FREE FOR ALL When the Holy Spirit hits our church we'll find that people we don't know will come in and start ministering to others. One church member came up to me once and said, 'I don't know who that fellow is, but he's already prayed for three women'. It can seem restrictive to say, 'We have a ministry team here. Don't let anyone pray for you who isn't wearing a badge.' But it's a safeguard to the flock. The newcomers who are praying for others may be genuine and we don't want to quench their gifts. But we do need to know who they are and who their pastor is.

PERSONAL PROPHESYING In their excitement some people try to prophesy beyond their gifting. Personal prophecy shouldn't be given by inexperienced people. We need to watch out for it and teach into it.

GENERAL FOOLISHNESS Drunkenness is foolishness, but sometimes it can go a bit far. Sometimes a person can just touch someone else and pass on the Spirit's laughter. But this can develop into silliness. Christians can go around with an 'I'll get you' attitude. We need to discern the difference between authentic holy drunkenness and just plain foolishness. We're not on holiday here. We're on a great mission — the salvation of the world. While we must embrace what God is doing, we must also take care that we're not being diverted from this goal.

Foolishness can come through insensitivity too. Many of those who are lying on the floor are listening to God. It isn't helpful if we sit or stand close to them and talk about yesterday's football match or what colour we're decorating the bathroom. They don't care about these things. All they want to do is hear from God. Let's either pray with them or move away so that we don't interrupt what God is doing.

FREE FOR ONE We believe in body ministry and need to release what God is doing to others. Let's avoid super spirituality and be naturally spiritual. God wants us to be down to earth in our friendships. Some people we pray for will immediately fall under God's power, others won't. I was praying for a woman and was wondering what was happening, so I asked her if God was saying anything to her. She replied, 'God is telling me that I'm like a strong oak tree.' How inappropriate it would have been for her to have fallen over!

On one occasion someone prayed for me in a meeting and God drew really close to me. I didn't fall over, I just stood there for a long time, soaking. I found the experience very informative. The people who came over, prayed and expressed love were the most helpful. The church leader came up to me and asked, 'Are you having a good time or a bad time?' That really impressed me. When we're ministering to others, we must be slow to speak God's words to them. Sometimes it's better to ask, 'What's happening? Does this mean anything to you?'

WEARINESS This move of the Spirit probably means that we're holding more meetings and might be tempted to be carried along by the busyness of it all. We must guard against living on meetings and their euphoria and maintain a close relationship with God.

ELITISM It's easy to think that we're the privileged few whom God is blessing. That's an elitist attitude. The reality is that the Spirit is moving across the board. We mustn't overstate things and claim that more is happening than actually is.

## Practical guide on prayer times

We need to understand what's happening so that we can properly evaluate it. I believe that when we lay hands on people God is refreshing and empowering them. They're opening themselves up to God and He's drawing close to them. The first time that the Spirit breaks out it's almost impossible to handle things. But as we continue to see God move, we need to take practical steps so that we can help people to get the most out of what's going on.

Physical space is a priority. We shouldn't pray for people unless there's space behind them and someone to catch them if they fall. They need to be relaxed to communicate with God, so it's no good ministering to them if their hopes are mixed with tension and anxiety, if they're thinking, 'What's going to happen to me if I fall backwards?' They need to know that there's someone to care for them and we must instruct our people in this.

We should encourage people to whom we're ministering not to pray along with us. Sometimes they feel that they've got to engage their intellect and speak in tongues. I usually tell them, 'I'll pray for you. You just receive.' We don't need to lay a heavy hand on them when we pray. That can be really off-putting, because they think that they're being pushed over. The catchers shouldn't be manhandling them either. A light touch on someone's back will say to them, 'Someone's here to catch you if you fall'. The catcher should stand fairly close to the individual so that if they do fall, they're carried all the way from an upright position to the floor. Let's be loving and caring in the way we handle people.

If people fall on the ground, let's encourage them to stay there and listen to God. The sense of His presence often grows in intensity, so if people get up too fast, they might miss what He wants to say to them. It's not important that people fall over. It's important that they receive from God.

Children need to understand what's going on in the meetings. I heard one church leader say to his congregation, 'If you've got your children with you, will they be frightened if you fall over? Do they understand what's going on?' We need to instruct the children and encourage parents to do the same.

When we've been praying for others a lot, we need to ask them to minister to us. That does two things, it replenishes our energy and it shows everyone that we're not setting ourselves up as special. Others need grace from God and so do we. I often find that when I've been praying for people I'm becoming weary and need to allow them to minister to me.

Let's not get so involved in what's happening that we fail to oversee the event. Someone must be in overall charge and have his eye on the microphone because things can go wrong.

Finally, let's set aside extended periods of time to pray together as leaders. We need a context in which we can be refreshed and receive the prophetic.

# An arrow for God

**TERRY VIRGO**

Isaiah watched his nation go downhill. Israel turned away from God and sank into idolatry and unbelief. There seemed to be no hope either for this nation, or for any others. Then Isaiah prophesied that there would be a deliverer, another Israel, a servant of the Lord who would come from the presence of God and bring that presence to the people. All christians know this servant's identity. He's the Lord Jesus Christ, the one who came bearing the full 'radiance of God's glory' (Heb. 1:3), the one who declared, 'Anyone who has seen me has seen the Father' (John 14:9).

In the Old Testament, God's servant is sometimes seen as an isolated individual and sometimes as a nation. New Testament eyes can understand this. Jesus is a person, but He's also the head of His body, the church. People who are 'in Christ' are God's servants and have His work to accomplish. That's why so many of God's promises to His servant in Isaiah are applied to us in the New Testament. Jesus is 'a light for the Gentiles' (Isa. 49:6) and we're 'the light of the world' (Matt. 5:14). Our lives are linked with Jesus' life. What is true for Him is true for us as well. So we can read verses about Jesus in the Old Testament and apply them directly to us today.

Speaking on Jesus' behalf, Isaiah said, 'Listen to me, you islands; hear this, you distant nations: Before I was born the LORD called me; from my birth he has made mention of my name. He made my mouth like a sharpened sword, in the shadow of his hand he hid me; he made me into a polished arrow and concealed me in his quiver. He said to me, "You are my servant, Israel, in whom I will display my splendour"' (Isa. 49:1–3).

God made Jesus His arrow and He wants us to be His arrows as well. An arrow speaks of being thrust out. It has a mission. And we've been called to follow the One who was thrust out of heaven for our salvation. Let's look at some of the characteristics of arrows.

### An arrow has to be made

A snowflake is complete in itself, a bulb brings forth a new flower and an egg produces a chick. An arrow differs from all of these in that it doesn't arrive fully formed or reproduce itself. It's made out of something that existed in another form before.

A disciple, like an arrow, has to be made. Before we're converted, we aren't automatically arrow-like. Quite the opposite, in fact. We have another shape altogether. Our roots are in the mindset of our generation and we don't get a new identity from birth, upbringing, or training, or by trying to add religion to what's already there. We've got to be totally severed from the empty way of life that was handed down to us from our forefathers (1 Pet. 1:18). We must find our new identity in Christ. As Peter said to Jesus, 'We have left everything to follow you!' (Matt. 19:27).

Even when we become christians, we're constantly being bombarded by another value system. Many of us may have been delivered from a lot of legalistic religious attitudes that made us feel condemned. But we must be careful not to tip the balance too far and return to the world for its entertainment or approval. The old carnal lifestyle is futile. It offers us nothing and won't help us to become effective arrows. Rather, it will hold us back from God's purposes and we must face this head on.

Young christians often adopt the world's values. 'Everyone's doing this kind of thing' they say. 'That's the way it is.' They've allowed the world to fashion their thinking, but if they want God to use them, they must review their attitudes — particularly to things like boy/girl relationships. It shouldn't be so much, 'How much can I get away with' as 'How much can I be transformed to look like an arrow rather than a branch?'

Sometimes we rely too much on the teaching that we've received in the past. We have career dreams and seek financial security from the world. Maybe we've been taught that to get on in life we need a good job, a big house and a smart car. But these are just natural desires. They aren't necessarily from God at all. Paul said, 'May I never boast except in the cross of our Lord Jesus Christ, through which the world has been crucified to me, and I to the world' (Gal. 6:14). He'd finished with his old life and was living from the new.

It's easy to play at christianity. We may be charismatic christians who are enjoying the current move of the Spirit. Maybe we're experiencing God's presence and power in the meetings. 'This is great' we think, 'It doesn't seem to matter that I'm a rather worldly christian. God is blessing me anyway'. God is gracious. He pours out His blessings on His people — even the uncommitted ones. But He wants to bring us to the point where we say 'OK, Lord. I give myself totally to You. I'm no longer looking to the world to meet my needs. From now on I'm turning my back on it. I want to press on and live a different kind of lifestyle from others around me.'

God made me in the first place and He isn't shocked at that. I was once a branch in a tree, but now He wants to change me into an arrow. He knows how He wants to do that, but He needs my co-operation. I've got to realise that the end times are approaching and that God needs arrows that are sharp in His hand. If I want to be useful to Him, I must be whole-hearted about cutting myself away from my previous lifestyle and leaving everything to follow Jesus.

This severing from the past appears in many places in the Bible. Abraham was called away from his roots, so was Jacob. Jesus left heaven's glory and took on another form so that He could be our Saviour. Do your friends or colleagues know that there's a radical difference in the roots of your life? Are they puzzled by the values that you hold or the decisions that you make? Have you given yourself to your new identity?

### An arrow has to be shaped
Once an arrow is cut away, it has to be shaped. An archer will see a long branch, slice it off the tree and then look at it

more closely. 'Yes,' he'll think, 'I can use this straight section, but I'll have to remove those twigs because they'll get in the way'. Those twigs are part of the identity of the branch, but they've got to go.

If we want to be God's arrows, we must be prepared for Him to cut away things in our lives which aren't arrow-like. Sometimes this pruning process will hit at the very roots of our identity. 'That's the sort of person I am' we'll say. 'Do I have to give up this relationship? Will I lose my friends?' The answer may be, 'Yes'. The way to life is narrow and if we want God to use us, we must co-operate with Him as He works in us. John says, 'Everyone who has this hope in him purifies himself' (1 John 3:3). It's not about loss, but about being shaped up to be purposeful in the plan of God.

Paul says, 'No-one serving as a soldier gets involved in civilian affairs — he wants to please his commanding officer' (2 Tim. 2:4). If I want to be an arrow for God, I must question what I'm doing with my time. I must ask, 'Is this helping me to be sharper for God or is it making me blunt?' Paul says, 'If a man cleanses himself ... he will be an instrument for noble purposes, made holy, useful to the Master and prepared to do any good work' (2 Tim. 2:21). That's the character of an arrow — it's sharp, polished, ready and available. The five virgins were like that — prepared for the bridegroom whenever he came to them (Matt. 25:1–13). We should be able to say, 'Yes, Lord. I'm focused, sharp, ready for You whenever You come to me'.

It's such a tremendous privilege — you feel like a useless branch on a futile tree. Then God sees you, cuts you off and says, 'I can see something worthwhile in you. I'm going to sharpen you, put you in My quiver and use you in My great plan to win the nations to Myself'. He'll put you through painful trials which will sharpen you, polish you and change you into what he wants you to be. F. B. Meyer said, 'Trials are God's vote of confidence in us'. God knows what He wants to do in your life. Are you willing to go through the pruning process in order for Him to accomplish it?

## An arrow needs a point

No matter how much you sharpen a wooden arrow, it will never be sharp enough. To penetrate defences, it needs a point which is made up of another element altogether. Archaeological research has unearthed many arrow heads, but no shafts. The shafts have long since disintegrated, but the heads remain.

It's not enough to say, 'If I'm as sharp as I can be, then I'll penetrate the enemy's defences'. The fact is that our best will never be sharp enough to slice into the hearts of those who don't believe in God. We need power from on high. Jesus said, 'You will receive power when the Holy Spirit comes on you' (Acts 1:8). When the power of the Spirit came upon the disciples at Pentecost, Peter preached and the people who heard him 'were cut to the heart' (Acts 2:37). The arrow found its mark — but it had a supernatural tip to it.

We can't prove the truth of christianity by our arguments or logic. We may wonder at the extraordinary signs we're seeing in our meetings. Why are people shaking, laughing or falling over? I think that one obvious reason is this: God wants us to depend on the power of the Spirit. In the past we may have thought we were doing just that. But then God does something unusual among us and we're saying, 'What's this? We haven't seen this before.' Surely, God is arresting our attention. He's telling us, 'You can't do this work on your own. It isn't just a question of your sanctification, your commitment, your desire to be separate from the world. You can't say, "If I'm as straight as I can be then I'll be successful". Only My Spirit will give you the power to penetrate and you must rely on Him alone.'

Paul told the Thessalonians, 'Our gospel came to you not simply with words, but also with power' (1 Thess. 1:5). Intellectual ability isn't sufficient, nor are speaking skills. We need a point which has nothing to do with the shaft. The Holy Spirit is foreign to us, which is why His activity seems so strange. He's described as wind and fire, and it's His power, not our sharpness, that will win the day.

In this current move of the Spirit God wants us to keep receiving from Him. We've been dry for years. We've often been relying on evangelistic activities to be the tip to our arrow, but it doesn't work. It's good to plan guest services and open airs, but they'll all fail unless the Holy Spirit is at the forefront of all we're doing.

When Peter was in Cornelius' house, he'd barely said anything before the Spirit fell on everyone there (Acts 10:44). And when he was confronted by a cripple, he said, 'What I have I give you' and performed a mighty miracle (Acts 3:6). This move of the Spirit has barely begun. Now isn't the time to be saying, 'Maybe this time of refreshing will fade away soon'. It's time to be crying out, 'More, Lord! We desperately need more!' We need to overflow with the power of the Spirit.

Why didn't Paul use wise and persuasive words when he preached the gospel to the Corinthians? Was it because he wanted their faith to rest not on men's wisdom, but on the Word of God? No — although many evangelicals would like to think that. He said, 'that your faith might not rest on men's wisdom, but on God's power' (1 Cor. 2:5). Certainly, the Word of God needs to have an important place, but the resting place for our faith must be in God's power.

Paul was a brilliant man. He learned the law from Gamaliel and excelled in ability above everyone around him. But he refused to let his preaching rest on his brilliance. He preferred to boast about his weaknesses, so that Christ's power might rest on him (2 Cor. 12:10). We've quoted verses like this for years, but I don't think we've known what it's like for power to break through. Now it's as though God is saying, 'This is a training house. Learn here and I'll do more and more among you.' We pray for one another and much to our amazement, the power falls. We need to be as straight as we can, but we're looking for penetrating power to do the job.

Even the perfect Son of God needed to be anointed with power. He said, 'The Spirit of the Lord is on me, because he has anointed me' (Luke 4:18). Peter told Cornelius' household, 'God anointed Jesus of Nazareth with the Holy Spirit and power' (Acts 10:38). Jesus was brilliant when He was twelve years old — as we can see from His conversation with the Rabbis in the temple (Luke 2:47). But He waited until He was thirty, until He was filled with devastating power. Then He went out and preached and healed. What must it have been like to go into town and see Jesus heal one person after another until there wasn't a sick person there? He had power. We've hardly got any yet. So don't think, 'I wonder how long this move of the Spirit is going to last'. It will continue until we have the power to do the job for Jesus. Paul says, 'The kingdom of God is not a matter of talk but of power' (1 Cor. 4:20). We must have more power than we do now.

Before the Israelites invaded the Promised Land, the Canaanites were terrified of them. What made them so afraid? Was it how nice Joshua was to his wife? No. It was the way that God dried up the Red Sea and destroyed their enemies (Josh. 2:9–11). Certainly, we need teaching on things like family life, but that won't ruffle unbelievers. What will make them sit up and take note is a mighty demonstration of God's power.

This power is added to us from the outside and it's a repeated experience. The early church received the Spirit at Pentecost and were filled again by the Spirit in Acts 4:31. We mustn't despise that. It's easy to say, 'I've already received the baptism in the Spirit and can speak in tongues'. Or, 'I was prayed for the other day, so maybe I shouldn't ask for more prayer'. God wants to shake us out of this way of thinking. Get prayed for again and again!

### An arrow has feathers

A friend of mine hunts grizzly bears with a bow and arrow. One day I asked him about the feathers and he told me, 'They're for balance, direction and stability'. The feathers don't naturally grow out of the shaft, they're foreign to it. And we need to add to our lives truth as it's revealed in the Word of God.

The Word isn't natural to any of us. Paul says, 'The man without the Spirit does not accept the things that come from the Spirit of God, for they are foolishness to him, and he cannot understand them, because they are spiritually discerned' (1 Cor. 2:14,15). We can't grow feathers from our own wisdom. They must be added from outside.

We must abandon our unbiblical ideas about God. Some people say, 'I always think of God like this. I couldn't imagine Him doing that sort of thing. It wouldn't be appropriate'. That's living from our own wisdom when we should be taking on board the inspired revelation of God. We can have the greatest power at the tip, but if we don't add the feathers, we'll go all over the place. Tragically, many people have done that. They've had incredible power but haven't had a balanced theology. As a result, they've gone off at a tangent. We won't accomplish much if we simply glory in the arrowhead. God wants us to get hold of the doctrines and give ourselves to truth.

The reformers brought orthodox theology back into the church. I read books by great teachers and they inspire me to worship God and get to know Him like they do. Then I see the people who are moving in great power and I want to imitate their faith. The trouble is that those in the 'theology camp' look at those in the 'power camp' and declare, 'Their teaching is off the wall'. And those in the 'power camp' look at those in the 'theology camp' and conclude, 'Their teaching is dry and stuffy'. It seems that 'never the twain shall meet'.

This state of affairs is totally foreign to the New Testament. Jesus taught truth and manifested God's power, and the early church abounded in both. I long to see orthodox theology working with the supernatural — that sharp tip brought together with wise balanced feathers. It's never enough to say, 'I've got the doctrine. I've sharpened my piece of wood. I don't need the power.' Nor is it sufficient to say, 'I've got the power. It doesn't matter about the theology. I'm just following the Spirit.' Let's bring them together. Let's study the Word and read books by great theologians, and let's experience the power of God and move out in it.

## An arrow has a quiver

You co-operate with God as He works in your life. You give yourself whole-heartedly to Him and He sharpens you. You think to yourself, 'I'm ready to be sent out', but God then confronts you with another challenge: He doesn't seem to use you. The polished arrow isn't immediately placed in a bow but plunged into a quiver. You're tossed around in there and you begin to wonder, 'What's happening to me now?'

God told His servant Moses, 'Come up to me on the mountain' (Exod. 24:12) and Moses obeyed. Did God speak to Him immediately? No. We read, 'on the seventh day the LORD called to Moses' (Exod. 24:16). What was Moses doing for the other six days? If we heard God saying, 'Climb this mountain' and did as He said, wouldn't we be thinking, 'OK, Lord. I'm here. You can speak to me now.' But if you're God's servant, you'll be happy whether He speaks to you on the seventh day or the twenty-seventh.

So you may think, 'I'm polished, I'm ready'. But God may reply, 'Right, into the quiver'. You may question, 'But I was made for a bow'. And God may answer, 'You were also made for a quiver. You're My servant and I'm your Master. I want you sharp and ready, but I'll tell you when you're going in the bow. I want to use you, not glorify you. It's not your battle, it's Mine. So you must remain in the quiver until I decide to use you.'

It's tough to hear these words. Delay often makes us discouraged. We find ourselves in a desperately hard situation and it's all slog. 'I never thought it would be like this' we think. 'I'm really not feeling fulfilled. When is God going to develop my ministry?' Paul might have said the same when he was in Caesarea. He was kept in prison for two years there (Acts 24:27). Why should God do that? Because that's what He chooses to do. We're His arrows in His quiver for His battle. He decides when He wants to use us.

So we go through tough times: we have problems with our job, our family, unemployment, the sale of our house, our health. We thought we were going for God, but we're restricted by trials and delay. These things seem like dark holes, but they're actually beneficial to us. They're part of the process of preparing us for battle. We want to be the sharpest we can, but God is sovereign and we're His servants. We're not here to exalt ourselves, to develop 'my name, my ministry, my career'. We're here to serve God. When God's greatest servant was twelve years-old, He was a match for the Rabbis. But He waited another eighteen years in that quiver in Nazareth before God shot Him into history. And we must wait.

The friend who hunts bears told me, 'The quiver isn't just a bag for carrying arrows. It's specially made to protect them.

It's the most important item that you have with you when you go hunting. You guard it, care for it and value it more than anything else. You don't carry it like a shopping bag, it's strapped to you so you can't forget it. It's vital for the battle ahead.'

The arrow inside the quiver thinks, 'This is just a dark hole'. But it's not. We're not concealed in any old bag, we're in God's quiver and it's the most precious thing that He's carrying. He tells us that He's loved us with an everlasting love (Jer. 31:3). We may not understand what's happening to us, but we mustn't throw away our confidence. We may be tempted to think, 'Lord, did I prepare myself so hard for this? It seems like a disaster.' God wants us to declare, 'Lord, I can't see the way ahead, but I'm trusting You. You've worked these things into my life and I believe that You're looking after me and will use me in Your time.'

An archer wants his arrows to be immediately available to him, which is why he straps the quiver to his body. It ensures that he never has to fumble around for an arrow. At any moment he can draw one out and shoot it. Paul wanted Timothy to be clean and ready (2 Tim. 2:21). We may think, 'My life is hidden from God. He's forgotten me.' The reality is your life is now 'hidden with Christ in God' (Col. 3:3). He won't discard the arrow that He's chosen and worked on. So be clean and ready. You may be amazed at the way that God will use you.

God knows what He's doing. Look at Joseph. God showed him that he'd be a leader and anointed him with the Spirit. As a slave in Potiphar's house, Joseph was committed to the truth and landed up in prison because of it. He remained hidden in God's quiver for several years, but God continued to bless him. Joseph kept the anointed point sharp — moving in the supernatural by interpreting dreams for others. Then one day Pharaoh had a dream and God reached for His arrow. Overnight Joseph became the central figure in history and began satisfying the hunger of the nations.

God wants to pull back His bow and send His people into the world. There's a target somewhere that He wants you to hit, and that's the reason why He wants you sharp and available. People need Jesus. They need to see the church come alive in their town, to see a people who are living by the Word of God in the power of the Holy Spirit. There's no hope for the world apart from a move of the Holy Spirit, and God wants us to be arrows — polished, sharp and ready to go.

# Praying for revival

**JOHN HOSIER**

Habakkuk 3:2 says, 'LORD, I have heard of your fame; I stand in awe of your deeds, O LORD. Renew them in our day, in our time make them known; in wrath remember mercy'.

We know nothing of Habakkuk outside his writings. But in these verses he's obviously a prophet of God who is standing before the Lord and praying for revival. The King James Version translates part of this verse: 'O LORD, revive thy work in the midst of the years'. Clearly what Habakkuk is asking for is revival.

Wise teachers of the Word will seek to understand the times and seasons that they're living in. When they sense what the Spirit is saying, they should speak into the situation as they perceive it. Now we're in a certain season in church life and I feel an urgency to address the subject of revival.

Much is currently being said about the so-called 'Toronto Blessing' which is sweeping around the world. I keep reading quotations by Jonathan Edwards who was probably the best philosopher that America has ever known. He wrote about the Great Awakening 250 years ago and we're seeing today similar phenomena to what were taking place then. This great revivalist leader is therefore able to help us to understand what's now happening.

Many churches are testifying to the blessing of God and there's increasing talk about revival. Some people have referred to this current move of the Spirit as revival. I personally wouldn't call it that. I believe that it's a time of refreshing which is coming mainly to christians. That's not to minimise what's happening. It's just to say that we need to be careful with our terms.

Some people think that this move of the Spirit is the precursor to revival. Indeed, church leaders in Argentina are looking at what the Spirit is doing around the world and saying, 'This happened in Argentina for five years, then revival broke out'. We mustn't lock ourselves into their formula, but it's good to be aware of their experience.

I've met some people and have wondered, 'Are they open to the possibility of revival?' Revival is about a great outpouring of the Spirit of God, which usually isn't neat and tidy. Maybe what we're experiencing now is getting us ready for further disruption when meetings are interrupted or extended according to God's plan. Perhaps we're being prepared to receive even greater blessing from God.

Habakkuk ministered about 600 years before Christ at a time of crisis in Israel's history. The Assyrians had overrun the northern territories and wiped them off the map. Only southern Israel remained — the small nation of Judah, whose centre was Jerusalem with its temple of God. There had been attempts at reform within the nation, but the people were backsliding and deserting the Lord in favour of idols. When a nation becomes godless, it always becomes unrighteous. Judah was godless, so sin was abounding and all sorts of despicable things were taking place.

We see unrighteous in our nation because it's godless. People try to improve the situation by suggesting all sorts of material or social things. Some of these may be helpful, but they aren't the answer. Better education might be a bright idea, but what we really need are more christians who will turn the nation back to God. Give people a better education and you'll get clever sinners. Introduce them to Jesus and you'll get new creations. When we're godly again, crime, violence and corruption will subside and there'll be an increase in righteousness.

We've fallen away from God. Every week I seem to hear about church members who have had their homes burgled or their cars vandalised or stolen. It's just a small part of what's happening in our nation. People are godless, so they're unrighteous. But when God pours out His Spirit in revival, the moral tone of any community is transformed. Courthouses have few cases to try and the judges have little to do.

Habakkuk struggled with the godlessness of his nation and he was told that things would actually get worse. God said, 'I am raising up the Babylonians, that ruthless and impetuous people, who sweep across the whole earth to seize dwelling-places not their own' (Hab. 1:6). The Babylonians wouldn't be raised up by chance. They'd be summoned by God to judge His people and reap destruction on the nation. This is the background to the conversation that the prophet now has with God. His words are very helpful to us as we look at the possibility of revival in our day.

### LORD, I have heard of your fame

Habakkuk doesn't begin with the problems in his nation. He starts by acknowledging the greatness of God. The Bible always begins with God because it's a God-centred book. Sadly, our generation tends to begin with man and focuses mainly on problem solving. Indeed, many churches are built on this philosophy. They feel that the priority is to discover the needs in society and work towards meeting them.

But the prophet begins with God. 'LORD, I have heard of your fame,' he says. The word, 'fame' embraces the holiness, majesty and glory of God. It acknowledges that He's from everlasting to everlasting, the One who created the universe and who is totally self-existent. That's where we begin when we're considering the subject of revival. We get our eyes off men and on to God. Compared to Him we're nothing — just a vapour that's quickly gone. Our problems may seem real enough, but they'll soon pass away, and so will our church buildings. Beyond everything there's a living and almighty God who reigns for eternity.

Above all, we need to acknowledge the sovereignty of God. Habakkuk was living among an ungodly and unrighteous people who in no way reflected God's goodness. Naturally, he was concerned for the nation, but he had to discover that

God wasn't going to rescue the nation at that time. Rather, He was going to judge it. That's the sovereignty of God and He will work in the way that He chooses, not in the way that seems best to us.

We can say, 'Please, Lord, send Your Spirit into our church, revive our nation'. But we can't give Him a programme to follow. We may pray, 'God, save the nation' but He might send in the Babylonians. The nation of Israel was eventually renewed, restored and revived — but that was many years down the track. God puts His plan into operation and because He's sovereign, we can't stand in His way.

### I stand in awe of your deeds

Habakkuk considered God's fame, then he focused on the history of God's dealings with the nation. Most of chapter 3 is a poetic account of the things that God did for His people — how He brought them out of slavery and across the Red Sea, how He destroyed their enemies and brought them into the Promised Land.

We aren't christians on the basis of some good ideas or philosophies, but on the basis of historical facts. Now some people say that facts don't matter. 'There's no need to think that Jesus was literally God made flesh' they say. 'He was just such a godly man everyone began to see Him like that'. Others declare, 'We don't need to believe in an actual resurrection. The resurrection really means that the life and ministry of Jesus live on in people's thinking.'

But there's no hope if what the Bible says actually didn't happen. If what it says isn't fact, then it's open to anyone's interpretation and we'll never be sure of any of it. We must understand that the Bible is a historical record. Jesus is God made man. 'Veiled in flesh the Godhead see,' wrote the great revival leader, Charles Wesley. Jesus brings God and man together. And on the matter of the resurrection, Paul says, 'And if Christ has not been raised, your faith is futile; you are still in your sins. Then those also who have fallen asleep in Christ are lost' (1 Cor. 15:17,18). If the resurrection isn't a historical fact, let's stop kidding ourselves that there's life after death and resign ourselves to hopelessness.

Our faith is based on historical facts. God has worked in history. Jesus Christ was crucified, buried and raised from the dead. He ascended into glory and will return for those who trust in Him. If our faith isn't rooted in what actually happened, we're deceived and may as well give up.

We also have the facts of church history. Eyewitnesses have recorded on paper what they've perceived of the church — both from a negative and a positive point of view. On the negative side, church leaders of 250 years ago were saying that church buildings were empty and that they were distraught at the state of the church.

### The eighteenth century
In 1736 one church leader wrote:

'It is come, I know not how, to be taken for granted, by many persons, that Christianity is not so much a subject of inquiry; but that it is, now at length, discovered to be fictitious. And accordingly they treat it as if, in the present age, this were an agreed point among all people of discernment; and nothing remained, but to set it up as a principle subject of mirth and ridicule, as it were by way of reprisals, for its having so long interrupted the pleasures of the world.'

*The Inextinguishable Blaze* by A. Skevington Wood, © 1960, The Paternoster Press.

Two years later, the Bishop of Oxford wrote:

'In this we cannot be mistaken, that an open and professed disregard of religion is become, through a variety of unhappy causes, the distinguishing character of the age. Such are the dissoluteness and contempt of principle in the highest part of the world, and the profligacy, intemperance and fearlessness of committing crimes in the lower part, as must, if the torrent of impiety stop not, become absolutely fatal. Christianity is ridiculed and railed at with very little reserve; and the teachers of it without any at all.' *Ibid.*

That was the state of the nation 250 years ago. Church buildings were empty, christian leaders and christianity were ridiculed, corruption and violence were rife. On 24th May 1738, John Wesley went to a meeting in London and received assurance of faith in Jesus Christ. On 1st January 1739, he prayed through the night with George Whitefield and others and the Holy Spirit fell on them with incredible power. That was the beginning of the mightiest revival that Great Britain has ever seen.

We need to consider our history from a negative standpoint. Our generation isn't uniquely different from others. We can't say, 'There's something special about us. No previous generation has had to face the problems that we've got.' Certainly, we've experienced some modern technical and scientific advance, but man has always been the same. And there have been many times when the state of this nation has been as bad as it is now — empty church buildings, people scoffing at christianity, wickedness everywhere. Then God poured out His Spirit and revival came.

The church in the UK hasn't declined slowly. It's had its ups and downs. At times, it's been a remnant people. The nation has deserted the places of worship, but a handful of believers have kept the flag flying. Then God has moved in and crowds have poured into the church.

In the eighteenth century God raised up Wesley and Whitefield and they led a great revival in England. John Wesley saw over 100,000 people come to Christ through his ministry. And George Whitefield, who was probably the greatest preacher that this nation has ever known, used to preach to crowds of up to 80,000 in the open air. Whitefield went to America seven times and was powerfully used in the Great Awakening there, alongside Jonathan Edwards. Both America and England were shaken to the core by the Methodist revival. Indeed, secular historians say that the moral climate in the UK was so changed that the nation was saved from certain revolution.

God works spontaneously in revival — often in churches that are outside the mainstream of things that are happening. William Grimshaw was an Anglican vicar in Yorkshire who spent his time hunting, fishing and playing cards. The only thing that could be said in his favour was that when he got drunk, he took care to sleep if off before he went home. On Sunday he would borrow a sermon from someone and preach it. Then his wife died and he began to seek God.

One Saturday in 1742 he prayed right through the night and into the next day and began to receive visions from heaven. He started the Sunday service at 2.00 p.m. and it went on until 7.00 p.m. One historian says,

> 'Thus Grimshaw passed out of death into life without help from any human quarter and quite independently of the great movement then afoot in the land.' *Ibid*.

Later that year he became the vicar of a tiny community in Haworth. His preaching there soon filled the church and Sunday sports were abandoned for lack of supporters. If we're concerned about Sunday opening, the way forward isn't new legislation from men, it's revival from God.

Grimshaw was so successful that people complained about him to the Archbishop of York, who summoned him to his palace and asked him how many were in his congregation on a Sunday. Grimshaw said that in winter there were 300–400, but in summer, nearer 1,200. The Archbishop was impressed, but following more complaints, decided to visit the church himself. Two hours before the service, he told Grimshaw what to preach on and then sat down along with several jealous ministers who were hoping to see the end of Grimshaw's ministry.

It was a mighty service and at its close, the Archbishop went over to Grimshaw and said loud enough for all to hear, 'I would to God that all the clergy in my diocese were like this good man'. From that time on, Grimshaw became a great evangelist in Yorkshire and an apostle to the north of England. He'd preach fourteen times in a lazy week and thirty in a busy one.

## The nineteenth century

In the nineteenth century there was a remarkable series of revivals which began in America, jumped across to Northern Ireland, to Wales and then into parts of England. This revival hit Wales in 1859. It wasn't led by outstanding men like Wesley and Whitefield who would probably have been great whatever they'd done. It was led by two ordinary people: David Morgan and Humphrey Jones. Morgan was described as a simple country pastor and for a time the two of them worked together.

One Sunday, in Tregowan, Wales, Morgan and Jones preached a sermon together. Many of the older members of the church were praising God and crying out jubilantly as if filled with new wine. When the two men held prayer meetings, conviction would fall on the congregation. People would weep, flee in terror, or stand rooted to the spot, not daring to move. Prayer meetings were also held in the coal mines. One meeting began at 6.00 a.m. and went on until 2.00 p.m. because the Spirit fell on the miners.

David Morgan had an amazing experience. One morning he woke up at 4.00 a.m. and realised that something extraordinary had happened to his memory. He could remember everything of a religious nature that he'd ever heard. Sermons that he'd preached or listened to came back to him in perfect detail. During the following months he found that he could pray for dozens of converts and their families by name and recall their exact circumstances, spiritual condition and the order in which he'd spoken to them. Two years later he woke up and the gift had gone. It was sovereignly given to him in a period of revival.

There were remarkable scenes whenever David Morgan preached— weeping, sorrowing, leaping and dancing. In one service, during the hymn before the sermon, people began to cry out under conviction of sin and continued to do so for two hours. By the end of that meeting there were thirty new converts.

In the six months from January to June 1859 many local congregations had increased by 200 members. This is how David Morgan records one particular story:

'In an evening service, a coarse and callous farmer was strangely affected. In the morning he was alarmed by the consciousness of a mysterious and revolutionary change in himself. *He was unable to swear* ... He sought his servants at their work, imagining that he would there find sufficient reasons for the exercise of his cherished habit, but for the life of him he couldn't rap out a single oath. Then he realised that his ailment required a drastic remedy, and he thought, as a last resort, that if he could see some neighbour's sheep trespassing on his pasture the lost faculty would be recovered. So he climbed a hill that was near, but nothing availed. He began to tremble

in every limb. 'What is this?' cried he. 'I can't swear; what
if I tried to pray?' He fell on his knees among the furze-
bushes, and continued a man of prayer as long as he
lived.'

This quote and statistics below are taken from *When He Is Come* by Eifion Evans, © 1967,
The Evangelical Press of Wales.

In that revival 110,000 were added to the churches in Wales,
whose population was far smaller than it is today. In 1897 it
was estimated that nineteen out of every twenty converts were
continuing well in local churches.

## The twentieth century

Early this century God called the Englishman, James Fraser
to minister to the unevangelised Lisu tribe in Western China.
He learnt the language and pioneered alone, living in appalling
conditions and travelling through areas which were full of
bandits. Food was sparse and he suffered from continual bad
health. As he went round ministering, one or two would
occasionally come to Christ and then fall back.

After six years God gave him the faith to believe that many
Lisu families would be saved. A while later, while he was
preparing to leave the area to minister elsewhere, he sensed
that his prayers had been answered. He could see no change,
but was confident that God was going to move. Before he
left he decided to make one final tour around the villages.
When he reached the first of these, 49 families came to him
and said, 'We want to become christians'. He met the same
kind of response wherever he went and within a few months
he had a church of thousands.

Sometimes we might be tempted to despair over the state of our church and nation. But we have the facts of history and need to look back and say with Habakkuk, 'I stand in awe of your deeds, O LORD'.

### Renew them in our day

Having looked at God's deeds in history, Habakkuk prayed that God would move in power in his day and bring a great awakening among his people.

When we pray for revival, we're not pouring out words into an empty sky. We're addressing the sovereign Lord who reigns and who's moved powerfully in history. We're calling on Him to do again what He's done before through people like Whitefield, Morgan and Fraser. We're asking Him to intervene again today.

### In wrath remember mercy

Habakkuk didn't pray, 'We've sinned and drifted far away from you, but now we're trying to do better'. He didn't appeal to the works or merits of men, but to the character of God. He acknowledged that God was going to pour out His wrath on Judah through the Babylonians — which He did. But he prayed that even though the people deserved God's wrath, He would temper it with mercy.

Do we feel that we're worthy of revival? I don't think so. We can't tell God, 'Look at what we've done. We're good enough for revival now.' The church is in a troubled state. So-called christian leaders are denying the divinity of Christ and the resurrection. And society has fallen into great unrighteousness because the church hasn't adequately proclaimed the truth.

Those of us in livelier churches could be tempted to become proud and think that we're a bit better and deserve a revival. But we have no claim on God. All we can do is come to Him, appeal to His character and plead that He'll temper wrath with mercy. Mercy is about not receiving what we deserve. And grace is about receiving what we don't deserve. So we must pray, 'God, bring mercy and grace. Don't deal with us as we deserve but show us Your power and revive us again.'

Our church and nation are crying out for change. There's only one answer. It's not better social workers, teachers, lecturers, or housing conditions — although all these have a part to play. We need God to break forth from heaven and transform us into godly people whose righteousness will exalt the nation to the praise of His name.

# Great expectations

**■■■■■■■■■■■■■■** JOHN HOSIER

We desperately need revival. We live in a day when churches lack faith in the Word of God and in God's power. Often there's an air of defeat and worldliness and things happen which reveal a complete misunderstanding of the nature of the church. I'm not against Trade Unions, but when vicars consider joining a TU to get better conditions for themselves, they're treating the church like a worldly organisation and not like the spiritual community that it is.

We rejoice that hundreds of new churches have been planted in the UK over the past twenty years, but we still need revival. New churches tend to be quite small and their impact on the nation rather limited. We need a mighty move of the Spirit to make any real headway against the powers of darkness that are at work in the land.

We only need to glance through some statistics to see that we desperately need a powerful move of the Spirit in the nation.

Let me give you some 1994 statistics.
Every day in Great Britain at least ...

470 babies are aborted.

20 women are raped.

400 couples are divorced.

90 children run away from home or care.

150 people are found guilty of drug offences.

## In addition:

One new crime is committed every 6 seconds.

A violent attack takes place every 2 minutes.

At least 65% of videos for sale or hire deal with the occult, sex or violence.

The pornographic industry is worth over £100 million annually.

Crime is costing British businesses more than £5 billion a year.

At this point it might be helpful to look at three questions on the subject of revival.

**What is revival?**

We need to know what revival is, otherwise we might end up calling something a revival when that's not what it is at all. First, I'll put it negatively. Renewal isn't revival. Renewal is something personal which speaks of a fresh encounter with God. Individuals become aware of His love and power in a new way. Many people have been renewed in this recent move of the Spirit. God has touched them, their lives have been transformed and they have a new desire to read the Bible, pray and witness. Naturally, we praise God for this.

Restoration isn't revival. While renewal is an individual experience, restoration is a corporate one. It's about getting whole churches sorted out and has much to do with structures (e.g. Ephesians 4 ministries). Certainly, we want to see the church restored to a New Testament pattern, but restoration isn't revival because we can get the church built on the right foundation, yet fail to see God's power. Indeed, some churches seem to have the power without the structures.

Revival is more than a personal or corporate experience. It's a community experience which radically affects both the church and those outside it. 250 years ago the revival hit the east coast of America. It was called the 'Great Awakening' because the churches were stirred from their slumber and communities were startled out of their sin and introduced to the Saviour. Jonathan Edwards and George Whitefield ministered during the Great Awakening. Here's a famous account of what happened when Whitefield visited a place called Middletown.

> 'Now it pleased God to send Mr. Whitefield into this land and my hearing of his preaching at Philadelphia, like one of the old apostles, and many thousands flocking after him to hear the gospel and great numbers converted to Christ. I felt the Spirit of God drawing me by conviction ... Next I heard, he was on Long Island and next at Boston and next at Northampton and then, one morning, all on a sudden, about 8 or 9 o'clock there came a messenger and said, "Mr. Whitefield preached at Hartford and Wethersfield yesterday and is to preach at Middletown this morning at 10 o'clock." I was in my field, at work, I dropped my

tool that I had in my hand and ran home and ran
through my house and bade my wife get ready quick to
go and hear Mr. Whitefield preach at Middletown and
ran to my pasture for my horse with all my might,
fearing I should be too late to hear him. I brought my
horse home and soon mounted the horse and took my
wife up and went forward as fast as I thought the
horse could bear, and when my horse began to be out
of breath, I would get down and put my wife in the
saddle and bid her ride as fast as she could and not
stop or slack for me except I bade her, and so I would
run until I was almost out of breath and then mount
my horse again, and so I did several times to favour my
horse ... for we had twelve miles to ride double in little
more than an hour ...

'We went down with the stream, I heard no man speak
a word all the way, three miles, but everyone pressing
forward in great haste, and when we got down to the
old meetinghouse there was a great multitude — it
was said to be 3 or 4000 people assembled together.
We got off from our horses and shook off the dust,
and the ministers were then coming to the
meetinghouse. I turned and looked towards the great
river and saw ferry boats running swift, forward and
backward, bringing over loads of people, the oars
rowed nimble and quick. Everything, men, horses and
boats, all seemed to be struggling for life, the land and
the banks over the river looked black with people and
horses. All along the 12 miles I saw no man at work in
his field but all seemed to be gone.'

*Jonathan Edwards, A New Biography* by Iain H. Murray, © Iain H. Murray 1987.

That's revival. It touches a whole community. Perhaps I ought to make clear here that evangelism isn't revival, although evangelism will spring from revival. In the United States people speak of holding a revival, but we can't hold revivals, God gives them. That's basically the difference between an evangelistic crusade and a revival: man does one, but God does the other.

I'm not knocking evangelism. It's Christ's commission to the church. Jesus didn't say, 'Go into all the world and have a revival'. He said, 'Go into all the world and preach the good news to all creation' (Mark 16:15). Even if there were no revivals in history, we'd still have the command to tell all the nations about Jesus.

One danger in teaching about revival is this: it can bring about a state of passivity. When people hear that revival is God-given, they can conclude, 'Well if that's the case, we can simply wait for God to move'. George Whitefield could have thought like that. He believed in the sovereignty of God but he was fervent in evangelism. He preached the gospel passionately and God swept thousands into the kingdom and performed many mighty signs and wonders.

With evangelism, it's the preacher who makes the appeal. With revival, the people do that. Suddenly they're convicted of their sin and cry out, 'What must we do to be saved?' Evangelism is ongoing. It's our commission to the end of time. Revival comes in seasons. God steps in sovereignly, awakens the church and draws large numbers of people to Himself.

## What will we see in revival?

No two revivals are the same. They vary in length, results and character. But they do have some things in common. One of them is conviction, which comes on those inside and outside the church. Although christians know that they've been forgiven and are righteous in Christ, in a time of revival they suddenly become aware of the holiness of God and are deeply convicted about their casualness, prayerlessness and specific sins.

Those outside the church come under a great conviction of sin and their need of salvation. In times of revival, unbelievers are desperate to get to christians meetings where they can find the Lord Jesus Christ. Sometimes people don't get as far as the meetings because God sovereignly convicts them wherever they are.

About twenty years ago a missionary was working in Natal, South Africa. His ministry was barren and he was so discouraged that he was on the verge of giving up. One day he was praying with a group of christians when a wind from heaven descended on them. Then out of the bush witch doctors suddenly appeared saying, 'What must we do to be saved?' God intervened, convicted these unbelievers and made them desperate to experience salvation.

This implies that revival touches our emotions. Some of us may be worried about that. It's often hard to know what to do when we see people upset. Certainly, tears can be of the flesh, but in genuine revival they'll flow freely because people come under such tremendous conviction.

Robert Murray McCheyne was the pastor of St. Peter's Church in Dundee, Scotland and he ministered from the age of 22 to 29 when he died. During those seven years a great revival broke out in his church — although he was in Israel when it began and a man called Mr Burns was leading the people. Listen to this account of what happened.

'On Thursday ... at the close of the usual prayer-meeting in St. Peter's, and when the minds of many were deeply solemnised by the tidings which had reached them, he (Mr Burns) spoke a few words about what had for some days detained him from them, and invited those to remain who felt the need of the outpouring of the Spirit to convert them. About a hundred remained; and at the conclusion of a solemn address to these anxious souls, suddenly the power of God seemed to descend and all were bathed in tears. At a similar meeting next evening, in the church, there was much melting of heart in intense desire after the Beloved of the Father; and on adjourning to the vestry, the arm of the Lord was revealed. No sooner was the vestry-door opened to admit those who might feel anxious to converse, than a vast number pressed in with awful eagerness. It was like a pent up flood breaking forth; tears were streaming from the eyes of many, and some fell on the ground groaning, and weeping, and crying for mercy. Onward from that evening, meetings were held every day for many weeks; and the extraordinary nature of the work justified and called for extraordinary services. The whole town was moved. Many believers doubted; the ungodly raged; but the Word of God grew mightily and prevailed.'

As this was happening, McCheyne returned from Israel.

> 'His people, who had never ceased to pray for him,
> welcomed his arrival among them with the greatest joy.
> He reached Dundee on a Thursday afternoon; and in
> the evening of the same day, — being the usual time
> for prayer in St. Peter's, — after a short meditation, he
> hastened to the church, there to render thanks to the
> Lord, and to speak once more to his flock. The
> appearance of the church that evening, and the aspect
> of the people, he never could forget. Many of his
> brethren were present to welcome him, and to hear
> the first words of his opened lips. There was not a seat
> in the church unoccupied, the passages were
> completely filled, and the stairs up to the pulpit were
> crowded, on the one side with the aged, on the other
> with eagerly-listening children. Many a face was seen
> anxiously gazing on their restored pastor; many were
> weeping under the unhealed wounds of conviction; all
> were still and calm, intensely earnest to hear ... After
> solemn prayer with them, he was able to preach for
> above an hour. Not knowing how long he might be
> permitted to proclaim the glad tidings, he seized the
> opportunity, not to tell of his journeyings, but to show
> the way of life to sinners.'

Both quotes from *Memoirs and Remains of R.M.M'Cheyne* by Andrew A. Bonar, © 1966.

McCheyne didn't come back and say, 'Here are the slides,
folks'. He knew that this was revival. God was moving
powerfully and people needed to be saved, so he preached

the Word to them. The whole community of Dundee was affected by that revival. And it involved deep conviction and emotion.

Another mark of revival is spontaneity. Revival isn't organised, it's God-given. Prayer meetings suddenly spring up and last for hours because people just want to pray together. Sometimes people are so convicted of their sin that they turn up at church buildings for services that haven't even been planned. The meetings don't go the way that man plans, but according to God's agenda.

During the Welsh revival of 1904, people used to come to the evening meetings with their lunches packed for the following day. That was in case the Spirit came down and they didn't get away from the meeting all night. Spontaneity brings with it a degree of untidiness and some excesses. When the spiritual atmosphere is highly charged, there will inevitably be some extreme and bizarre behaviour which will need to be checked. Jonathan Edwards said, 'We should distinguish the good from the bad and not judge the whole by the part'. Revival is about life, and life is untidy. If you want it neat and tidy, go and sit in a cemetery!

Although signs and wonders aren't confined to revivals, we'll see them in revivals and they'll vary in intensity from revival to revival. In the Welsh Revival Evan Roberts was given a vision of a piece of paper on which was written, '100,000 souls'. He took this to heart and prayed for that many new converts. During 1904 and 1905, 100,000 people were added to the churches in Wales.

We'll also see community impact in revival. In 1904, the police in Wales said, 'Things are easy for us now'. I'm sure they aren't saying that where you live! But in Glamorgan, convictions for drunkenness in 1903 were 10,528 and in 1905 they were 5,400. Even the pit ponies couldn't understand the orders that they were being given because the miners were no longer swearing at them. Revival has an amazing impact on the community.

## What can we do to prepare for revival?

When Solomon had built and dedicated the temple, God promised him, 'If my people, who are called by my name, will humble themselves and pray and seek my face and turn from their wicked ways, then will I hear from heaven and will forgive their sin and will heal their land' (2 Chron. 7:14). I can't give a foolproof way to revival, but I think that this Scripture gives us some clues about how to prepare.

For a start, we must be serious about it. God says, 'If my people'. He's looking for people who will seek Him about the desperate situation in their nation. I joined a Baptist church when I was fifteen. Later, I trained in an evangelical Baptist college and led two Baptist churches in different parts of the UK. I lectured at an evangelical Bible college for three years and have been an elder in one of the Restoration Churches for eight years. In all those years I've certainly heard people praying for revival, but I don't think I've ever sensed a great and sustained seriousness about it.

Seriousness about revival will be demonstrated by several things. The first is humility. God says, 'If my people who are called by my name, will humble themselves'. We must recognise our utter dependence on God. Our greatest sin is pride, and pride kept us from God in the first place. We thought that we didn't need God and could manage without Him, but we couldn't. Now that we're christians, we could be thinking, 'I've recognised my need of God, so pride isn't my problem any more'. But we are prone to pride because we can live as though we don't need Him.

Some years ago I was challenged by this question: 'Supposing you had a Bible beside your bed and while you were asleep one night, someone came along and deleted every reference to the Holy Spirit. What difference would it make to your christian life?' We must recognise our need of God.

To be provocative, I'd like to suggest that most churches in the UK have reached their present size because of the skill of their leaders. They may be good churches with real spiritual qualities and excellent Christ-ordained leadership. It's just that their growth is largely attributable to the gifts and organisational abilities of those in leadership. But when revival comes, things are different.

A few years ago there was a revival in Argentina. Before it came, many pastors were leading churches of 200–300. Then almost overnight, they were faced with congregations of 2,000–3,000. This had nothing to do with their skills, abilities and giftings but with a mighty intervention from heaven. Certainly there is a place for organising our weekly courses, evangelistic activities and housegroups. But what we really need isn't better organisation or new ideas, but a mighty breakthrough from God.

James Fraser had that breakthrough. For years he was working among the Lisu people and seeing very little fruit. Then suddenly he had a church of thousands. This wasn't the result of his ability. God came in revival power and totally reversed the situation. We need to humble ourselves and get rid of our pride. Our nation is in desperate need and our only hope is in the living God.

Another mark of seriousness is repentance. God calls His people to 'turn from their wicked ways'. Now we can't set up a formula for repentance. Charles Finney was a great revivalist in the USA in the nineteenth century and many thousands came to Christ through his ministry. As he preached from town to town, people were overcome by a sense of God's holiness and their sinfulness. As they repented, revival came. When Finney saw what was happening, he began teaching that repentance would lead to revival. He was actually setting up repentance as a method and that can lead people into terrible bondage and legalism. People can begin to submit to the method to avoid the criticism of others rather than respond to God out of personal conviction. Legalism doesn't produce revival. It produces death.

So, while revival is always preceded and accompanied by repentance, repentance doesn't guarantee that revival will take place. Christians get serious with God and confess their faults to one another. They set things right with others in the church and want to live a truly holy life.

A number of missionaries were working in Korea at the beginning of this century. They weren't having much impact on the community and when the Japanese invaded, the missionaries called the christians together to pray. The Spirit fell on church after church. Believers were prostrate on the ground under conviction of sin and there was a great deal of public confession. The school teachers couldn't continue with their lessons because the children were confessing their sins to each other. Huge prayer meetings were started up at four or five o'clock in the morning. These continue even today. So without trying to nail down a formula, I'll simply point out that revival is commonly preceded and accompanied by repentance.

Seriousness is also reflected in prayer. God says, 'If my people ... will humble themselves and pray and seek my face'. This sort of praying isn't casual, it comes from the heart and it's persistent. I wish that I could give you a revival prayer formula — something like, 'If we all prayed for two hours every night for two months, God would send revival'. But it doesn't work like that. The closest thing that we have to a formula is found in Luke 18:1: 'Then Jesus told his disciples a parable to show them that they should always pray and not give up'.

Revival comes when people seek God's face and pray. Evan Roberts, leader of the 1904 Welsh Revival said, 'For ten or eleven years I have prayed for revival and in 1904 heaven opened and revival came to the province of Wales'. Some people think that prayer is the key to revival, but it isn't. We can pray for months and waste our time because we haven't humbled ourselves and repented of our sin. There's no basis for God to answer us. If there's one thing worse than unanswered prayers, it's long unanswered prayers. We must get serious, turn from our sin and pray. Then God will hear us and heal our land.

Revival is our greatest need. It's also our greatest hope. God will not leave the church in her apparently forsaken condition. We don't want to despise small things, but we're still struggling, still making little impact, still seeing few conversions and still subject very much to the skills and organisational ability of the leaders. But the Spirit is moving.

Our hope is this: that the God who has intervened throughout the decades of human history will respond to the cries of His people. Our hope is that suddenly heaven will open and He will shake the church and awaken us to our need. Our hope is that He will break into our community, transform lives and bring a mighty revival to our generation.